2/99

DOES AMERICA HATE
THE POOR?

DOES AMERICA HATE THE POOR?
The Other American Dilemma

Lessons for the 21st Century from
the 1960s and the 1970s

John E. Tropman

Westport, Connecticut
London

Library of Congress Cataloging-in-Publication Data

Tropman, John E.
    Does America hate the poor? : the other American dilemma : lessons
for the 21st century from the 1960s and 1970s / John E. Tropman.
        p.   cm.
    Includes bibliographical references and index.
    ISBN 0–275–96132–X (alk. paper)
        1. Poor—United States.   2. Poverty—United States.
    3. Discrimination—United States.   I. Title.
    HC110.P6T76   1998
    305.569′0973—dc21   98–11135

British Library Cataloguing in Publication Data is available.

Library of Congress Catalog Card Number: 98–11135
ISBN: 0–275–96132–X

First published in 1998

Praeger Publishers, 88 Post Road West, Westport, CT 06881
An imprint of Greenwood Publishing Group, Inc.

Printed in the United States of America

Contents

Preface

As we approach the twenty-first century, an examination of elements of the passing century may help us plan better for the future. So much has changed since 1900 that it seems almost a completely different world. Almost nothing we think of as "modern"—cars, planes, medical care, electronics—existed to any degree in the early 1900s. The Social Security Act, signed August 14, 1935, in its now twenty titles, provides help for those in need—the elderly, mothers and children, the unemployed, those with disabilities. It is a different world.

The more things change, though, the more they seem like the same things. While we provide help for the needy, the poor, and the old, we are deeply suspicious both of "them" and of "helping them." Themes articulated as the century closes about the poor, their need to work, and the unnecessary benefits they receive are much the same as those articulated as the century opened. Historically, the thinking was that if "poverty" was bad, "pauperism"— accepting help for being poor—was worse. It destroyed the individual's independence. As Rauschenbusch commented, "To accept charity is at first one of the most bitter experiences of the self-respecting workingman. Some abandon families, go insane, or commit suicide rather than surrender the virginity of their independence. But when they have once learned to depend on gifts, the parasitic habit of mind grows upon them, and it becomes hard to wake them back to self-support" (1911, 238).

Almost seventy-five years later, a *New York Times* article by Frank Levy announced, "A Growing Gap between Rich and Poor" (Levy 1988). And shortly after that, a headline for the "Week in Review" section, July 28, 1996, shouts, "The New Contract with America's Poor: Get a Job!"

This book explores a dislike of the poor themselves and helping them, and seeks to understand it. Two specific groups of poor, the underclass (or status poor) and the elderly (or life cycle poor), are the main focus. Data about how people think about them, including how they think about themselves, are drawn from the period between 1960 and 1970, just past the middle of the century and the heyday of the Great Society, a period when rights of all kinds were being transformed from rhetoric into "reality." The War on Poverty was being waged in cities across the land. If attitudes toward the poor, underclass, and elderly, were more positive, this is the time period we should have seen some evidence of it. On the contrary, attitudes seemed suspicious and troubled. We were moving ahead, but not happy about it. On the one hand, we want to be helpful to those in need, and often are helpful to them. On the other hand, need frightens us, and all too often we wind up blaming the victim (Ryan 1971).

Why should this ambivalence be so? Why should we have a welfare state and a poorfare culture? The reasons are many, and entangled. If issues of race are one "American dilemma" (Myrdal 1944), then issues of the poor are another.

Obviously, considering the amount of ink the poor get and the extent to which the poor are regularly a part of the public discourse, the poor are deeply, perhaps uniquely, disturbing to the American psyche. They represent, perhaps even to themselves, themes contrary to deeply held values in American society, values which, of course, they themselves hold as well. Somehow, poverty is danger. But to what? Or to whom?

One answer to these questions lies in the importance of the issue of control in American culture. The United States is, if voting with your feet is a measure, the country of choice worldwide. In spite of our problems, people across the globe are dying (sometimes literally) to get here. America offers hope for upward mobility. American society is an open society, where "opportunity is our most important product." But if one thing the open society means is that you can ascend in status, it also means that you can descend. What goes up, socially, does not necessarily come down; but it can come down. And one never knows when that might be. This possibility is especially worrisome where social status is concerned. One member of a focus group shared the following perspective: "Living in American society is like living on the gong show! You think things are going great, but your head is always looking around. You never know when you are going to be gonged. The price of freedom is, well, no security at all."

And there is the rub. The hope that the open society offers has an underside, a threat, if you will. It is that anxiety—the anxiety of downward mobility—that means control is so important (May 1976).[1] The status poor embody this result.

A second reason may lie in the pressure for social exploitation. Because societal wants and needs always exceed available resources, most societies always live in the fear of, and on the brink of, going broke. Societies "balance their books" through processes of social exploitation, or forcing members to contribute their labor for free or cheap. Many calls for rights are really calls for an end to social exploitation. America has heeded that call, and we are now faced with the need to pay for, or pay more for, that which we had enjoyed for free or cheap in the past. Children, soldiers, and the environment are all costly to treat well. The need to pay for the rights we have now made real (or somewhat more real) is creating pressures for fresh social exploitation. The status poor and the life cycle poor are good potential targets for exploitation, and that process has already begun, has intensified, and will intensify in the future.

Here is one example. Peter Passell, writing in the *New York Times* on July 7, 1996, talked about the problem of "You Saved but They Didn't. So Now What?" He deals with the tension between the baby boomers who saved and were thrifty, and those who were not.

Here's the nightmare. You've socked away every stray penny in retirement accounts, resisting the temptation to live it up in order to accumulate a comfy nest egg. Now its payoff time: Hawaii beckons. But all the aging spendthrifts—the folks who bought fishing boats instead of mutual funds—persuade Congress to tax your savings and cut your Social Security in order to spread the wealth. A far fetched prospect in the home of the free and the land of the 401(k)? Don't be so sure. For while the baby boom generation's slowly building retirement crisis could be resolved in a variety of ways, punishing the thrifty will always be a tempting option. (Sec. 3, p. 1)

Whatever the reasons for nervousness about the poor—and there are obviously more and different ones than those suggested here—dealing with poverty and its relief is a central American dilemma. We have a welfare state encapsulated within a poorfare culture. The welfare state refers to the money we spend, the support we provide for those called "poor." Poorfare culture refers to our dispositions about doing it. The culture and the structure live in contradiction to each other. It is one of the cultural contradictions of Capitalism.

Like all important dilemmas, it is important in its own right and for what it can tell us about ourselves, our aspirations, our pasts, and our futures. Like many other dilemmas, it is not to be "solved" or "resolved," but rather managed and handled. Understanding is a good first step. I have tried to provide an interpretive explanation for what is going on. Perhaps Geertz's observation is appropriate here: "Interpretative explanation . . . trains its attention on what institutions, actions, *images, utterances,* events, customs . . . all the usual objects of social scientific interest, *mean* to those whose institutions, actions, customs, and so on, they are" (Geertz 1980, 167, emphasis added).

THE PLAN OF THIS BOOK

The purpose of this volume is to provide an opportunity to consider in depth why American society thinks and feels so negatively about the poor and the old as two categories of individuals. Some of the reports are from the poor and the old themselves, but all members of society are represented in the data. Chapters 3 and 4 focus on "images of the poor" and provide some information on how respondents in Boston and Kansas City in 1972 thought about those in poverty. Chapter 5 discusses responses from a national survey from about the same time on attitudes of county welfare directors. That study reflects not only the directors' own attitudes, but also their perceptions of the attitudes of the general public. Chapter 6 shares data from a Detroit area study (a survey of Detroit residents mounted every year by the Department of Sociology and the Institute for Social Research at the University of Michigan) in the mid-1960s. Here, a random sample of Detroit women were asked about public and private agencies, whether they had used them, and what their opinion was about them. Chapter 7 reflects upon images the elderly have of themselves and uses some data from a Louis Harris poll. Chapter 8 extends that investigation and blends in some nonscientific data from a popular magazine in an attempt to assess common factors as well as differences. Chapter 9 considers value change over time, between 1952 and 1978, using data from the National Election Study.

These data have interest to us for several reasons. First, they present a diverse set of assessments on a common theme. Second, all of the assessments were taken during the active period of the welfare state, between about the mid-1960s and the mid-1970s. Despite policy attention to both groups at that time (especially the elderly), there remained a substantial negativism. In addition, there does not seem to be a great deal of difference among varying groups of respondents in their negative perceptions of the poor. Thus, for example, respondents in Boston and Kansas City talk about differences between "the lowest class" or welfare class, as they tend to define it, and the "next to the lowest class," or working poor or decent poverty stricken.

The welfare directors (of local departments of welfare) felt themselves value isolated (having values not supported by others in the group) in a sea of hostility and negativism toward themselves and others from a national sample. It is little wonder that, in the "welfare reform" of 1996, many of these offices will have been resized, downsized, rightsized, and totally transformed.

Older adults share with younger adults, a few cultural and ethnic exceptions not withstanding, negative characterizations of elder status. The pictures from plenty are not as positive as we might hope. Indeed, they are so negative and, at times, hostile that the welfare state is not, after all, the appropriate term. The poorfare state is a more appropriate name. It is one of ambivalent attitudes and moralistic overtones, which tends, finally, toward blame and fault. This name—poorfare state—more realistically describes our thinking about the elderly and poor members of our society during the 1960s, the very time when policies toward both groups were in an expanding period.

NOTE

1. All societies are not like this. Some, like English society, operate more on a "ratchet" principle than a "greasy pole" principle. Turner (1960) calls this sponsored and contest mobility. In a ratchet society, you sort of "click in" to your status, and thus do not really use it.

Acknowledgments

Many people contributed to this book over the years. It is impossible to mention them all. Readers, editors, typists, each has made his or her contribution. Richard Coleman made the Boston and Kansas City data available. Henry Meyer made the Detroit data available. Rosemary Sarri made the county welfare directors data available. Roxanne Loy typed, and retyped, both text and tables. Barbara Hochrein spent many hours on the bibliographic material.

Special thanks go to a group: sundry students in the Joint Program in Social Work and Social Science at the University of Michigan. They read countless drafts, trashed many, but out of the ashes of each came a better, more focused document. Carla Parry deserves special mention. She worked tirelessly on the ideas and the structure of this book. Her suggestions for both detailed improvements and conceptual clarifications were outstanding.

Special kudos go to Rick Lane. Rick is a minister, a social worker, a clinical psychologist, and an information specialist. He is also a book lover and editor. Rick worked with me on the final preparation of the manuscript. His emmendations always enhanced, always improved, and always enriched.

I want to mention Msgr. John McCarran of Pittsburgh, and Rev. Thomas Harvey, CEO Emeritus of Catholic Charities USA. Both have retained patience through long conversations about the poor. We explored questions like, "Who are the poor?" "Why are they always with us?" "Why do we think the way we do about them?" and "Could it be different?" Their perspectives were humane and enriching.

To my children—Sarah, Jessica, and Matt—I owe an apology. Many are the vacations where I worked on this (usually in the mornings) when I should have been playing with them. They were, up to a point, understanding, but always supportive.

Finally, I own a huge debt to my wife, Penny. Her questions—"Why do some have more and others less?" and "How can we live with the kinds of discrepancies we see today?"—propelled me to think about the poor in their several aspects. And without her support, this document would not have been completed.

DOES AMERICA HATE
THE POOR?

Part I

WHO ARE THE POOR, AND DOES AMERICA HATE THEM?

For purposes of this book, I would like to talk about two groups of poor. One is the status poor, people in "the lowest class and the next-to-the-lowest class." The second group is the life cycle poor, or elderly. For different kinds of reasons they both present problems to the core values of American society: lack of a future and a reminder that "there, but for the grace of God, go I."

THE STATUS POOR

Consider that in American society—indeed, in most societies—there are five "goods" that people seek: money, power, information, status, and a job or occupation. Assume, as well, that in American society each of us ranks in a quintile on each of these variables. The following hypothethetical stratification system of five key vectors might illustrate this:

Quintile	Money	Power	Prestige	Information	Occupation
80–99	A	B	C	D	E
60–79	B	C	D	E	A
40–59	C	D	E	A	B
20–39	D	E	A	B	C
00–19	E	A	B	C	D

This would be a great society indeed. Everyone occupies one top spot, one bottom spot, and one spot in-between. It is a society that has, simultaneously, differention and equality.

But let us suppose that society is not so perfect. There are some people who have more of the "good things of life," and some who have a concentration of fewer of them. For purposes of argument, let us say as well that the vast middle is broadly distributed. A more or less open society would be one in which each of us was distributed in various positions within the cells. Some would be high in money, low in power, have only a fair job, and so on.[1] Elites would be those individuals who occupy several (let us say three or more) positions in the top row. The mass are most of us distributed in the middle three quintiles. A diamond would illustrate this system.

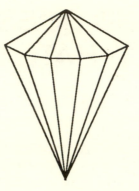

But perhaps some individuals are low on everything. There is some distribution, but there is a concentration of one group—the Es—at the bottom.

Quintile	Money	Power	Prestige	Information	Occupation
80–99	A	B	C	D	A
60–79	B	C	D	A	C
40–59	C	D	A	B	B
20–39	D	A	C	C	D
00–19	E	E	E	E	E

In this formulation, the poor are those (opposite of the elites) who are identified as being packed in the bottom quintile, with some combination of poor or no job, inadequate money, and little power, education, and status. These are the lowest class. Being low on all the totem poles is status poverty.

THE LIFE CYCLE POOR

A second group of poor are those in life cycle situations we find troubling. The elderly are such a group. Why? Aging represents, for most, losses and accommodations to those losses. Loss of life, of course, is the most obvious, but there are also loss of loved ones, loss of job, loss of the ability to do what one could in the past do, and loss of financial and physical control.

From another perspective, aging can be seen as the loss of a "future," of opportunity. If the process of life is a process of the development of personal capital, then the aging process is the process through which we need to pay the opportunity costs we have amassed, when it is, for most practical purposes, too late to do anything about it (whatever the "it" is).

All cultures do not approach aging in this way, of course, but America is a "young" country, with "young" people who can "get ahead." The foibles of the young are tolerated—young drinking drivers, young criminals, young this and young that—while the perils of the elderly driver are seen as requiring legislative action. With a few exceptions, no one who talks about restricting the young male driver or raising the age of driving, though recent changes found in some states, most notably Michigan, have added driving limitations on the basis of age and driving records. Problems of medical care for the elderly are discussed in terms of some extraordinary burden, while other burdens (young male criminals, for example) are almost passed off.

Perhaps the poverty of the elderly can be summed up by thinking about a loss of independence, of freedom. Who does not know of an elderly person who has not given up driving, moved to a retirement center or community, or entered into an assisted living arrangement? These are all cases that highlight the loss of independence and freedom. Aging represents life cycle poverty.

DO WE HATE THE POOR?

Status poverty and life cycle poverty represent two of perhaps many kinds of poverty. Those at the bottom of the stratification ladder and the elderly are, as a group, the poor considered in this book. The question then, is, "Do we hate them?" My answer is yes: not in the same degree, but for similar reasons.

Suspicion of the status poor, the "underclass," the "needy," the "homeless," emerges in virtually every discussion of them. This suspicion, concern, or hate often seems heavily involved with negative moral judgment. Americans often morally disparage the poor. There is the frequent reference to people in need as "them." "They" of course implies an "us," and it is only a half a step or less from "them and us" to "we're okay and they're not okay." Such a view is, perhaps, behind the epilogue chapter in Katz's (1989) study of "the undeserving poor, called 'Them' or 'Us.'" We hate others than the poor—hate crime and hate speech testify to that—but there are plenty of hate crimes and hate speech directed toward the status poor and the life cycle poor as well.

In 1996, with the signature of President Clinton, "welfare as we know it" (Aid to Families with Dependent Children; AFDC) ended, and the states took more control. The PRWORA (Personal Responsibility and Work Opportunity Reconciliation Act) ended AFCD and replaced it with Temporary Assistance for Needy Families (TANF). It does not take a weatherman to see which way the wind is blowing here. Beneath, and just beneath, all the talk is hate and fear of the poor.

The poor, then, are actual representations of what could happen to us, what will happen to us. We hate them not because they are us ("We have met the enemy, and he is us"), but because they could be us, or will be; because they represent features of the open society in operation we do not like; because they represent a truncation of opportunity and costs coming home to roost; and because we need their resources for our own use and feel guilty about it. Poverty is the embodiment and the realization of our fears.

NOTE

1. There are social thinkers who assert that one of these dimensions is primary and all others follow from it. Karl Marx, for example, felt that occupation was central. C. Wright Mills, in his book *The Power Elite*, felt that power was central. Others feel that power brings money, that money bring power, and so on. For our purposes, let us assume that each is substantially independent of the other and that the empirical question centers on the degree of crystallization, defined as the extent to which an individual occupies the same quintile on one, two, three, four, or even five of the variables. A 20-percent crystallization would mean having the same position on two of the variables; 30 percent on three, and so on.

Chapter 1

How America Hates the Poor

American society is a land of plenty. Foreign visitors I show around are astounded by many things; few, though, more than the supermarket. The typical supermarket has thousands of products. Almost nothing exemplifies the idea of choice, and the supply of goods and products that choice requires, than strolling up and down the supermarket aisles. (One visitor asked, incredulously, "Do you Americans really need more than two dozen kinds of toothpaste?") Visitors' eyes bug out—thousands of choices, and the products among which to choose. This is America.

It is, perhaps, the presence of choice—or the perceived presence of choice—sometimes called "opportunity," which becomes central to American views of the poor. American society is charitable worldwide, provides vast amounts of aid to developing countries, and tries with a missionary's zeal to get other countries to accept its point of view and values. Typical, perhaps, of reformers and exemplars, is that our own support of our own needy, within our "domestic system," to use Montgomery's (1976) phrase, is not as enthusiastically and positively endorsed as our actions in the world community would suggest. Somehow need "out there" is different from need "in here." That is because the poor out there do not threaten us as do the poor in here.

If my visitors are astonished at the supermarket, they are struck dumb by the pet-food aisle. As one guest said, "How can you have a whole aisle of dog and cat food, and have such hostile attitudes toward the poor. You treat animals better than people."[1] America's thinking about the poor is doubly revealing, and becomes an indirect observation on the central core values of American life. It becomes what Barbara Tuchman (1978) called "A Distant Mirror."

"Hate" may be too strong a word. But then again, it may not. It has a lot of synonyms: abhor, aversion, disgust, antipathy, rancor, malevolence, to name a few. And none of these words seem terribly out of place when applied to the poor. If "hate the poor" is a bit of hyperbole, it cetainly points in the right direction. Better to err in the direction of the problem than to cover it up. If we do not hate the poor, we certainly act as if we do.

HOW DOES HATE WORK?

How does hate work? Stigma, of course, is the first answer. What are the intellectual constructs that allow for the poor to be stigmatized, or promote such stigmatization? This question is an important one. One answer is that the poor person (or the Jew, or the Asian, or the Native American, or whoever) becomes, intellectually, linguistically, and emotionally, a "lessperson," and then a nonperson. Wolf Wolfensberger (1972) asked it in this way: "How can you treat people in ways that you would not treat people?" His answer is that you cease thinking of them as people. Rather, they become animals: "You rat!" "You pig!" "You dog!" "You son-of-a-bitch!" "You ass." One could add worm, weasel, cow, bug, (out)fox, and so on. The language of animalization presages and legitimizes the process of victimization. It is the same with the poor. Intellectual processes make it not only okay to hate the poor; we do not even think of it as hate. And this approach is among the more obvious. Invalidation of personhood occurs in more widespread and insidious ways as well, and each opens the way for inhuman actions. After all, you need not be humane to a nonperson.[2]

There are a number of other mechanisms that sustain poor hate as well. I have identified ten; there are doubtless more.

Mechanism 1: Values Dualism

Values are ideas to which commitments are attached. They represent an important way that people think about life events, from the most important to the most mundane. "Ways," the plural, is an important operative word. We have many values in America. Perhaps it is more accurate to think of "value dimensions," dimensions within which there are contradictory individual values, something Bell (1976) calls the "cultural contradictions of American capitalism," and the welfare state in particular (Tropman 1989).

We encourage and celebrate achievement, on the one hand, yet trumpet equality, on the other; we espouse competition, yet laud cooperation; we feel fair play is the way to go, yet we long for fair share as well; we lionize the mountain man, yet appreciate the wagon train; we support performance measures, yet support tenure and seniority as well; pay for performance clashes with across-the-board increases. We are in favor of self-reliance (each tub on its own bottom), but support "a hand in need"; we are compassionate, yet seek punishment; we celebrate "independence" (do not wear seat belts if you do not want to), but do not really want to let people deal with the consequences of their choice. We celebrate rights, but also worry about responsibilities. And so it goes.

Conflicts within the American value system create a slippery slope for thinking about the poor. Commitment to one does not mean we do not value the other; rather, it is question of dominance and subdominance. The fact that we favor and savor the accomplishments of the individual does not mean we are not appreciative of the efforts of the team; the mountain man does not drive out the wagon train. It is just that we favor the mountain man, and we favor the individual. It is more like 60–40, or 70–30, than either–or.

Being poor and being old are culturally dissonant states, and, as such, need to be explained, accounted for, interpreted, and dealt with. In some sense, poverty and aging may embody what Elaine Cumming (1967) called "anti-values," or what J. Milton Yinger (1982) might have called a countercultural state.

Consider the following list of values:

Dominant	Subdominant
Achievement	Equality
Fair play	Fair share
Competition	Cooperation
Self-reliance	Interdependence
Individualism	Community
Do it	Prevent problems (planning)
Equity	Adequacy
Youth	Aging
Mobility (up)	Stability (in one's station in life or job)
Contest	Sponsorship
Zero sum	Non–zero sum

The problem is that support for the poor, and support for helping the poor, must lie on the subdominant side of the American value system. The more we think positively about the poor, the more we need to rely on values that, while we believe them, we are not as strongly committed to as majority values.

Mechanism 2: Subdominant Values as Threats

Not only do the poor require us to upgrade subdominant values, but because of the linked nature of values pairs, emphasis on one threatens the

other. Hence, the poor are a values threat. Perhaps, in part, attitudes supportive of helping poor citizens conflict with other, more dominant attitudes, ones
involving suspicion of the victim, caution, tough love, and a "you-get-what-
you-deserve" mentality. There is plenty of "wiggle room" within the value
system for hating the poor. As you look at the list of values, note that while
we want the values in Column 2, we do not want too much or too many of
them. By their presence and their needs, the poor call out for more of the
subdominant values than the dominant culture is confortable with, indeed,
than the poor themselves may be comfortable with. Consider a common re-
frain of the senior citizen: "I do not want to be a burden!" Can readers imagine a teenager saying that? In this respect, the poor become a threat.

Mechanism 3: The Importance of Values of Mobility and Youth

There are some dominant values which are especially important as one
thinks about hatred of the poor. One of them is "getting ahead"—success. We
all seek it; we all want it. For some, of course, it is more important than for
others, but with the exception of a few individuals who, for reason of con-
science, religious affiliation, or other kind of group membership or commitment explicitly eschew it, "success," the wish for it, the search for it, the
demands for it, remains central to the American dream.

Success can take a variety of forms—usually along one of the five dimensions mentioned—much money, much power, a great job, high status, high
education. Achieving in one is good, several is better, and all at once is best.
Succeeding is the process of upward mobility. There are two stages. One is
intergenerational mobility, the sense that one is doing better than one's family of origin at the same adult age. The second is intragenerational mobility,
the sense that one is progressing along an upward slope in one's own career.
The truncation of both these kinds of mobility in the 1980 to 1990 period, as
we shall discuss more fully, was one of the reasons why the river of hostility
toward the poor, always present, overflowed into negative actions in the late
1990s. Whichever kind of mobility one thinks of, success is a master goal
(Tropman 1976, 1989; Rischin 1965).

There is a second image that fights for prominence in our thinking as well:
the image of youth. America is a young country. The immigrants, in most
instances, tended to be young people. To do something when one is young is
almost certainly thought to be better than doing it when one is not young, or
even old. Youth is widely thought to be synonymous with innovation, energy,
a fresh approach, and so on. Even "young" companies (such as McDonald's
or the computer companies) are likely to attribute part of their excellence to
that youthfulness. At the same time, it is mentioned that the "older" companies (steel, automobile manufacturing, railroads) are in trouble and founder-
ing (Peters and Waterman 1982). Youth, of course, may be and doubtless is an
important and desired good in its own right. But it implies and permits a path

of success available to you, a range of possible achievements and goals which are yet to be attained.

Mechanism 4: Hatred of "Dependency"

Successful and upwardly mobile are qualities the poor are perceived not to have. What the poor are perceived to be is "dependent." As a society founded on independence, any status which suggests the systematic reliance upon external forces for personal support and functioning is likely to be considered a dissonant state (Fischer 1978). Dependency tends to mean not only the needing of help but the accepting of help. Overreliance on programmatic help such as AFDC is often seen as an indicator of such dependency (Perlman 1960).

Michael Lewis (1978, 133), in his study of "Middle City," reflects some of these attitudes and perspectives. One of his chapters is titled, "Those people! They're just no good; they live off the hard working people; they don't care about their families; they're drunk; they're always causing trouble—they're getting away with murder." This theme of moral judgment is picked up by Handler and Hasenfeld (1991) in their book *The Moral Construction of Poverty*, and Michael B. Katz (1989) uses the phrase *The Undeserving Poor* as the title to his study of the journey "From the War on Poverty to the War on Welfare." Race is a factor, but poverty is the dominant condition. Lewis comments:

There are people in Middle City who never miss an opportunity to remark on the personal inadequacies of the poor, and particularly the black poor. . . . Arnold Stallings (a justice of the peace) has been accused of discriminating against black defendants who appear before him. In point of fact he does not do so. He does, however, treat poor defendants—black and white—in a manner that can best be described as paternalistic. . . . Poor persons appearing before Justice of the Peace Stallings are very soon made to feel that their future depends not so much upon the impersonal and principled workings of the law as on Stallings' personal sense of rectitude. (1978, 144–145)

Needing help is problematic in this tradition. Sometimes, though, accepting help is even worse than needing it. There are views which suggest that providing help makes people more dependent:

Poor persons seeking help will have to contend with Miss Mary Cloud, the sixty-year-old welfare assistant, who, while sizing up the applicants, harbors the assumption that unless she guards against it, they will perpetrate frauds against the interests and taxes of the good hard-working people of Middle City. They will have to convince her that they are not only really in need, but also that they are worthy of any assistance—no mean task because Mary Cloud believes, as she puts it, that, "welfare has become a way of life for many people who come in here." (Lewis 1978, 156)

There is certainly some truth in these thoughts and views. But it is the perspective they illustrate, the suspicion and hesitancy to help, that is worth noting.

In some sense, the culture of achievement may create a situation in which the poor threaten the nonpoor. Lewis speaks of the gap between achievement and aspiration in the Americans of Middle City as corrosive to their very sense of self. "What do they do about these threats to their self-worth? What do these good Americans do about this sense that whatever they have achieved, they have achieved too little?" (Lewis 1978, 134). If achievement is everything, then lack of achievement must be something to look down upon, if only to reassure the viewer that he or she is still "somewhat okay." And when you feel that you have not achieved enough, that your position on the ladder of accomplishment is nowhere near what you had hoped, helping someone below you becomes a tougher task. The poor then threaten the nonpoor because, in their asking for help (their very presence is an "ask"), the nonpoor may need to use that which is "theirs" to help those who may soon be their competitors.

For the older adult, of course, the need to be dependent in a variety of ways can become endemic. One might have health problems, causing physical dependency, limited mobility, or incontinence. One might have neurological problems or Alzheimer's disease, in which mental rather than physical loss is central. Less dramatic types of infirmity often limit the older adult's ability to function on his or her own. Talcott Parsons (1979), shortly before his own death, argued that older adults fear death less than disability and its inherent limitations.[3]

In sum, the realities of dependency which inevitably occur for the older adult and the poor person lead others in society to connect these states in a cause–effect association. This heightens our fear and negativism in regarding the status poor and the life cycle poor among us.

Mechanism 5 : Blame the Victim

One of the ways that threats are dealt with is to blame those who cause them. Ryan (1971) has outlined our penchant for this kind of thinking in his book, *Blaming the Victim*. Victims make us uncomfortable. We might have had some responsibility there. If something can happen to "them," it could, perhaps, happen to us. If however, it is their (his or her) fault, then we are more psychologically safe, we think. We will never do that, so the results of that will never bother us. Hating the poor serves, in a way, to allow us to love ourselves, or at least feel "okay."

Mechanism 6: The Language of Ambiguity

The values conflict which permeates American attitudes toward the status poor and the life cycle poor is amply evident in the ambiguity of language used to refer to individuals experiencing these conditions. The multiple meanings and connotations of the words poor and old reflect the ambiguity inherent in each of these postures and the reluctance of Americans to decide how we really feel about these conditions of life. Consider the word "poor" as a case in point. It is often used to mean "deficient in money," but it can also refer to a deficiency in quality. A poor job, a poor term paper, and so on suggest casualness and carelessness, resulting in quality below an acceptable standard. Here, with respect to the idea of below standard, the quality notion and the money notion link together. Speakers can shift or flit among these different definitions, stating one and implying the other, and in general evoke responses common to both definitions while purporting to use only one. Yet another use of "poor," meaning "sad or pitiable," adds a further dimension to the idea of poverty. Not only does it reflect a deficiency in money and in quality, but it is also to be pitied. Discussions of poverty can thus include all these different meanings, drawing upon an implication here and making an allusion there as needed to reflect the biases of those present (Himmelfarb 1983, see especially Chap. 1).

Now let us consider the life cycle poor, the elderly. The word "old" is often used, yet it too is a vessel full of ambiguity (Fischer 1978; Achenbaum 1978). Old can be simply used to mean advanced in years, but it is often more than a neutral descriptor. A statement such as, "She acts so old," is usually a negative reference, unless the reference is made to a young child, and there is a sense to be conveyed of maturity beyond chronological age, in which context the same formerly negative connotation becomes positive. By and large, however, it is not only chronological age but infirmity, lack of sense, and lack of ability to act properly, that is communicated by this use of the word old. Old can also mean familiar or comfortable, as in "old boy," or "old Harry," in which sense the word implies conventionality, and perhaps dullness.

The use of old in referring to an individual is often further qualified by the adjective "retired." When one is old, one retires, or does one? Retirement conventionally means leaving paid employment and possibly securing a pension as a result of that employment. But this word also has other meanings which confound the ambiguity already present in relation to the use of the companion adjective old, as we have seen. Notably, retire also means to go to bed, hardly thought of in general terms as a precursor of high activity and energy output. The word retiring also indicates a state of being shy, of holding back, or of not giving forth full effort and energy. Another use for the word retirement comes from the detective story genre, in which "to retire" is to execute, to kill, to be dead.

All of these multiple meanings provide some sense of the scope of the ambiguity which surrounds our references to the status and life cycle poor in American society. We equate poorness and oldness with, at times, lack of money, lack of quality, lack of energy, sadness, ineptitude, and even death itself. We might expect statuses so dissonant from acceptable and sought-after positions in America would evoke a complex of referents. It does, and not only about the statuses themselves, but about the causes and correlates of these statuses as well. Ambiguous language allows us to avoid truly confronting our feelings in an intellectual way.

Mechanism 7: Disengagement and Ghettoization

Another mechanism of hate is disengagement, a pulling away from the individuals in question. Given the nature of such pervasive disregard, it is no surprise that the poor suffer from disengagement. One theoretical formulation about disengagement of the elderly by Cumming and Henry (1961) suggests the elderly have a tendency to engage in a process of gradual withdrawal from social interaction, perhaps as a preparation for death. Subsequent efforts by social theorists to gather more data in support of this phenomenon have not really produced enough evidence to substantiate the theory of disengagement. However, it may be the youth who are disengaging from the old, rather than the other way around.

Disengagement from the poor is, however, immediately evident. There is a sense of social distance and distancing. After all, it is each of us, no doubt, who avoid eye contact with the homeless and quicken our pace to hurry on by them. The poor do not mingle with the suburban country-club set. They cannot afford it.

Disengagement is facilitated by physical separation. Both the status poor and the life cycle poor tend to live in "their" areas. The status poor live in slums; the elderly live in "senior centers." In both cases there is an exclusion, and it is often argued (on top of everything) that it is for the ghettoized person's "own good." Paraphrasing the rabbi in *Fiddler on the Roof*, "May the Lord bless and keep the poor—far away from us!"

Mechanism 8: From the Center to the Periphery

The tendency toward disengagement complements the observation that the poor and the old occupy peripheral statuses within contemporary American society. Edward Shils (1975) talks about social structures as having a center and a periphery, having major focal values and institutions as well as those more on the edge of the society. It is not suggested that those on the periphery are unimportant or trivial, but rather, less important and less central to the society, at least at a particular point in time. It is crucial to emphasize points in time, because over the passage of time in life or on a particular day, different structures, institutions, and values can become predominant.

The poor are accorded peripheral stauses which go with their peripheral geography. Indeed, evidence for their near invisibility is that special efforts need to be made to include them in civic processes. The concept of maximum feasible participation of the poor (Moynihan 1969) is a case in point; it recognizes the likelihood that poor individuals do not participate much in making decisions about programs which affect them, and tries to enlist the poor into more positive decision making. Senior centers likewise aim to provide places for older adults to interact with each other and with younger people who come there also. Despite social policies (welfare policies and policies of assistance to seniors like the Older Americans Act) aimed at reducing their peripheral position, there remain many ways—access to goods and success, and access to esteem and positive regard, to give two examples—in which the old and the poor are still on the outside looking in. This is one reason why Estes (1979) says that policy toward the older adult has been a failure. Anyone who has participated in meetings involving the poor will agree that they are mostly sham. (One meeting of a highly educated group of seniors began with the pledge of allegiance—shades of grammar school!)

Mechanism 9: The Target of Social Policy Attention

One definition of social policy might be that it is for those whom we fear.[4] The poor and the old have been the target of a lot of social policy. This policy ink alone suggests they are a problem. For some purposes they are combined, for others these groups have received separate attention. With respect to a common focus, surely the Social Security Act with its several titles dealing with both poor and old ranks first and foremost (Achenbaum 1983). One title of the Social Security Act deals with old-age pensions, survivors, and disability insurance. Another deals with medical care for the older adult. Still another provides medical care for the poor, and others provide for AFDC, now called TANF.

There have been other social policy efforts to deal with both of these groups that have not necessarily joined the groups together. The Economic Opportunity Program of the 1960s, and indeed the entire poverty program, could be seen as something which dealt with the poor and the disadvantaged (Moynihan 1969). On the other hand, the Older Americans Act and the Age Discrimination Act focused on concerns specific to the older adult (Estes 1979; Lammers 1983; Butler 1975).

Mechanism 10: Disesteem and Stigma

The existence of these culturally dissonant and negative attributions toward the life cycle poor and the status poor results in a degree of disesteem and distancing. It is in this area that cultural and historical differences can be most clearly etched, particularly with respect to the older adult. Language again makes a difference: geezer, coot, old bag, dirty old man, and many others reflect the operation of stigma.[5] On the other hand, there is no reason in particular why the older adult should not be venerated and cherished in the United States. After all, he or she has made a lifetime contribution to the society. In fact, the older individual is regarded as a repository of wisdom and perspective in some countries, such as Japan, as Palmore (1975) points out in his book, *The Honorable Elders*. The Japanese have approached the age structure with the sense of esteem rather than negativism (Plath 1980). A similar age-related deference was more characteristic of American society in the past. The intellectual historian David Hackett Fischer (1978) and social historian W. Andrew Achenbaum (1978) both point out the developing disesteem in American society with respect to the older adult.[6] The nature of our society, with its youthful orientation (points discussed earlier), may suggest that esteem for the older adult may never have been all that high, particularly when we compare it to other countries.

Disesteem for the poor has historically been both more constant and clear-cut in this country than abroad (DeSchwenitz 1943; Himmelfarb 1983). American society in particular seems to take a vigorous and militant negative posture toward the poor. Indeed, societal disregard for both the old and the poor in America is a fact of life.

Similarities between status poor and the life cycle poor are striking. For one thing, the elderly are growing in number. Much like the social security tax itself, there was limited notice of the elderly in 1935, when there were 6.1 percent over sixty-five (Darnay 1994); in 1995 seniors were more noticeable, when there were 12.7 percent over sixty-five[7] (U.S. Bureau of the Census 1996). The poor also seem to be more noticeable. Homeless individuals accost pedestrians everywhere, it seems. And the widespread attention to the middling out of America, with two groups, one rich and one poor, has received a lot of attention.

Both groups seem to accept definitional negativism with respect to themselves. Note, for example, an older individual who speaks pejoratively of "those old people." Status poor often talk about "the poor" as if it were some other than themselves.

Both groups, as noted, experienced social policy advantage, driven by the same piece of legislation. The Social Security Act of 1935 encompassed both the life cycle poor, some elements of the status poor (children and later mothers with children and still later unemployed families with children), the blind, and, later, the permanently and totally disabled.

A further indication of stigma is that people seek to not look poor or old. Going hand in hand with the ambiguity indicated by such verbal multiplicity and choice is the idea that you do not have to look poor or elderly, whatever that may mean. Clothes, manner, and presentation of self can create an image of okayness. Thousands of beauty parlors attest to the constant efforts and dollars spent in looking better, which means, generally speaking, looking younger. In spite of campaigns undertaken in formal literature and more popular magazines to convince us that the older ages are not by age alone devoid of advancement and fun, we dread the advance of years. In a success-driven and youth-oriented culture, where you can never be "too rich or too thin," being old and/or poor is not only a state or condition, it is also a process of becoming which is unbecoming. The least the poor can do is look like "us."

Indeed, in Michael Harrington's (1962) book, *The Other America*, a section entitled "Our Invisible Poor" points out that it is very difficult, at least using public, face-to-face criteria, to separate the poor from the rest of us. We hate them for reminding us they are not like us (and that someday—any day—we may not be like us either). We hate them and fear them for reminding us that they are us after we lose a job, or become ill, or "something happens." The similarities may scare us as much as the contrast. After all, there, but for the grace of God. . . ."

CONCLUSION

These ten mechanisms are the vehicles for how America hates the poor: (1) the problem of values dualism, (2) the threat of subdominant values, (3) the stress on mobility and youth in American society, (4) America's hatred of "dependency," (5) our ability to blame the victim, (6) the use of slippery and ambiguous language, (7) the application of disengagement and ghettoization, (8) the relegation of the poor to peripheral statuses, (9) the application of social policy to the poor, and (10) the presence of disesteem and stigma. Certainly, these interact and support each other, each strand strengthening the choking social rope.

I do not think that there is much question that America hates the poor. Some readers may quibble about the word "hate," and argue for something softer. Others will argue, "Well, there are exceptions—this group and that group," and in that process engage in "categorizing the poor," something we have done for hundreds of years seeking to create "exempt" categories of groups who are poor but okay.

But even if one accepts the general ideas that we hate and fear the poor— perhaps especially if one accepts it—questions pop up. How can we understand this? If we hate the poor, why do we spend so much to help "them." Are there, or is it too bizarre to consider, positive functions to hate? Perhaps the poor are always with us because we need them.

NOTES

1. He may be right. The first child abuse case was brought through the New York City Society for the Prevention of Cruelty to Animals.

2. One could add the principle of vegetablization, one step below that of animalization. In vegetablization, as in the phrase, "He is just a vegetable now," the distinction between life and death has been finessed. After all, you cannot really kill a carrot.

3. Disability may be an "advanced" death.

4. The word "social" itself has multiple meanings. One is collective, the social good; another is interactive, as in "social disease"; a third seems to refer to stratification, deprivation, and status poverty, as in "social problem"; and then, of course, there is "social policy."

5. One often hears infantilizing language used toward the poor as well.

6. They differ on the timing of its occurrence (Fischer locates it in post-independence America), and they differ as well on the reasons (Fischer sees ideas of independence and freedom as important, Achenbaum sees social changes in the workplace requiring greater manual strength as important). They both agree that disesteem and negative stereotypes have developed with respect to the state of the older person. The view presented in this analysis is that disesteem may not represent as pronounced a shift as both Fischer and Achenbaum suggest.

7. Figure adapted from 1930 and 1940 reported data.

Chapter 2

Poorfare Culture, Welfare State

American society has a social culture (value system) and a social structure. One is a system of beliefs and values; the other a system of policies and actions. Each clearly influences the other, yet the cultural aspect of American society can be characterized semi-independently from its structural aspect. In this respect, these results suggest that we have a poorfare culture in a welfare-state context.

WELFARE STATE

At one level there is no significant dispute that American society has moved into the league of "welfare-state players." Certainly, the hundreds of billions of dollars of public money which is spent to provide social assistance of one sort or another is ample testimony to this fact. Dear (1989, 27) points out, "More than $17 billion will go to eligible low income families in fiscal 1990."

When one includes the large number of other programs of social assistance, including social security and programs for the elderly, and adds to those federal programs for veterans administration, a substantial amount of the federal fiscal dollar is already marked for the entitlement programs to the disadvantaged and elderly. In addition to these tax-funded programs, other billions are made available through charitable contributions and expenditures in what is often called the voluntary sector (Tropman and Tropman 1987). To these significant numbers one can add welfare-state expenditures paid for directly by the private commercial sector through employee assistance programs and other private social welfare programs set up through business and industry. And we cannot forget the 10-percent discount for senior citizens that many establishments provide.

POORFARE CULTURE

It is clear that America is a welfare state. However, it appears to be a reluctant welfare state, a point that Jansson's (1988) book, *The Reluctant Welfare State*, has made as well. The trends on the structural level do not receive the kinds of support on the cultural level in the area of beliefs and values that one might like or expect.

On the cultural side, American norms and values, as discussed in Chapter 1, are generally negative and hostile with respect to the public welfare system. Poverty is still a morally problematic category and accepting help for being in poverty is even worse. Each generalization obtaining today was true during the 1960s heyday of War on Poverty activities, the period of time specifically considered by this book. The significant growth of social welfare activity during that period was not matched by similar growth in social welfare values. Indeed, the more we do, the more suspicious we get. Welfare reform, peaking in "ending welfare as we know it" in 1996, represents, in the eyes of many, a victory of hate and the triumph of the poorfare state over the welfare state. It is for this reason that the argument which separates poorfare culture from the welfare state makes some sense. Perhaps we have erred in trying to explain the "whole" rather than looking at the two parts.

Poorfare culture seems to be a negative, hostile view toward those at the bottom of the economic ladder, tinged with a special degree of disaffection from what observers judge to be a lack of effort, trying, or "keeping at it" of those in that economic position. An important suggestion of these results is that it is not specifically being at the bottom of the economic ladder solely which Americans seem to dislike, it is being there without "working." Working in this context must be understood not as having a job in the literal sense, for that would probably satisfy some of the objections, but as failing to evidence effort, put forth energy, or try. It is not to say that these perceptions are necessarily accurate. Individuals who have studied the disadvantaged point to the level of effort they put out just to survive on a daily basis (Stack 1974). Nevertheless, this perception creates a reality of its own to which other aspects of the culture inevitably respond.

Older adults are seen in a similar way. Here is where the negative patina of "retiring" comes into play. Retiring is "nonwork." What seems to be celebrated are the older persons who "keep at it." When I became head of the Institute of Gerontology at the University of Michigan, one of the programs that was already underway was a conference/show celebrating "the older achiever." It struck me, "Does it ever end in our society? Can we ever take a day off?" Yet there is another side. We want seniors to step aside so younger people can have top jobs. Typical of one who is hated, seniors are damned if they do and damned if they don't.

THE PROTESTANT WORK ETHIC

Why does our culture focus as it does on effort and activity? Where does the emphasis come from? What functions does it serve? One answer may lie in our historical dependence on the Protestant ethic. It is important to understand with respect to the Protestant work ethic that in America it was the dominant ethic; other ethics—a Catholic ethic or a Jewish ethic—followed, but those who founded this country were carriers of the Protestant ethic (Ahlstrom 1972). In Europe, a Catholic ethic was dominant. Catholic orientations and perhaps Jewish ones may be more supportive of welfare support than the Protestants (Tropman 1986).

The popular concept of the Protestant ethic has always been associated with the emphasis on work and activity. Its context and reference points have been that work was of a sacred nature—all work was God's work—and that success in work indicated God's favor. However, there may be a dark side to the Protestant ethic as well. Part of the very hostility toward the disadvantaged may come from this very same ethic. Its emphasis on material wealth as an indicator of spiritually positive character necessarily creates a negative by-product. Lack of material wealth indicates impoverished moral character and value. Indeed, it is this emphasis or theme which provides many discussions about the poor as well as many research reports reflecting data about them that somehow they have copped out, fallen short, or are not only financially disadvantaged but perhaps morally disadvantaged as well. Unusual as it may seem, the very values that have positive aspects have negative ones as well. Of course, almost any product, service, activity, or belief has an "upside" and a "downside." No one finds these assertions surprising until one applies them to sacred values. B. F. Skinner (1971) found this out in his well-known book *Beyond Freedom and Dignity*, in which he questioned some of the values encompassed in those words. The Protestant ethic, with its positive emphasis on work and activity, creates a negative emphasis on the disadvantaged and the poor. If work activity and money are going to be symbolic of positive moral achievement, then its absence is problematic. One might even say that one does not have full citizenship in American society unless one works, for pay. This is very troubling to many citizens. Women, for example, who may be at home caring for children respond, "I'm only a housewife," when asked, "And what do you do?" The disabled and retired have similar concerns.

WELFARE STATE IN POORFARE CULTURE

Overall, then, major contemporary American values and the American value system is historically not one that is sympathetic to the disadvantaged or to the poor. Rather, it is one which is hostile and suspicious of them. These aspects of culture are powerful, long standing, and have taken firm and deep root in Americans' belief systems. One might ask, however, in this value system, how did the welfare state come about if the poorfare culture is so powerful?

Cultural Pressures Supporting the Welfare State

There are two different types of answers to this question. One has to do with values. The first, as already noted, is that values are not all of a piece (Tropman 1989). Values are contradictory in and of themselves, and with other values. Specifically with respect to the Protestant ethic and its lack of sympathy toward the disadvantaged and the poor, there are contradictory ethics, exemplified by the Salvation Army, the Quakers, Lutheran Social Services, and so on.

Second, there are competing ethics of a religious-based nature which articulate other perspectives—especially a Catholic religious ethic—and which take a rather different and more positive position (Tropman 1986). It has been suggested by a number of my colleagues that there is also a very positive "pro-welfare" Jewish ethic (Rothman 1989). In *The Catholic Ethic in American Society* (Tropman 1995), some of the elements of the Catholic ethic and the ways in which it thinks about the disadvantaged (more like us than them) are detailed and supports help for those who need it as a natural thing to do.

In general, therefore, values conflict within and among themselves, and the fact that there is a darker side to the Protestant ethic involving negativism and hostility toward the disadvantaged does not mean that this is the only value held in this society, or that people who hold this value do not have other contradictory values within themselves.

One answer, then, to the question of how a welfare state can exist within a poorfare climate is that the poorfare climate is neither uniform nor totalitarian. Negativism exists, and it is a strong—I think culturally dominant—force in America. However, other cultural forces exist as well, ones that support welfare-state activity.

Structural Pressures Supporting the Welfare State

In addition, though, there are important structural pressures moving us toward the welfare-state posture which are independent of the culture to a great degree. The first of these, and often discussed, is the Great Depression. Many authors of social welfare texts point to the Great Depression as the beginning point for the welfare state in America via the passage of the Social Security Act and the other social legislation which characterize the use of public and governmental administration. There is certainly no question that the extensiveness and depth of the Great Depression was a major structural shock; people were thrown into situations which they had not experienced before, in which they were unable to cope, and which clearly were unrelated to any fault on their part. The Great Depression actually provided countervailing structural pressures for activity involving the welfare state in two rather different but related areas. Welfare itself was one.

Whether state run or not, welfare had never been terribly popular in American society for some of the reasons described. However, the legitimacy of the need transcended the historical opposition. In addition, the gigantic nature of the problem in need required a gigantic response, mobilizable only by government. Historically, American society had been antigovernment. After all, the country was founded by people who had fled from government oppression. It was baptized in the revolution against the potential for the reestablishment of that oppression. It is not surprising that Americans would view government activity with suspicion, and when one considers government activity particularly in relationship to welfare, resistance must have grown exponentially. Nevertheless, the Great Depression created a set of structural conditions that worked powerfully to overcome the historical resistances.

Structural change was not the only factor operating here. Some degree of cultural change was correlative with the structural pressures. After all, we had had depressions before, and, as has been pointed out by a number of authors, we have had "welfare" programs (the Freedman's Bureau and the Civil War Pension Program) which, unlike most government programs, were not continued, but rather actively disbanded. In addition to the structural pressure of the Great Depression, the cultural pressure of the Catholic and Jewish ethics (Tropman 1986) taking prominence if not dominance was a factor as well. Attitudes which supported the disadvantaged and which looked sympathetically rather then judgmentally upon their plight had come to the fore. The profession of social work itself is a representation of this increased concern.

The government action on a large scale stimulated by the Great Depression was followed almost immediately by another large-scale government program which involved millions and millions of Americans in a psychologically encompassing cause of high moral value from which a great success was produced, despite numerous serious problems and difficulties in the accomplishment of that success. This government program, of course, was World War II. In some respects it represents a strange but not illogical extension of the social programs of the 1930s. Now it was not just the poor who were on the government payroll; everybody was on the government payroll. World War II demonstrated that a large scale public effort could be mounted, could be a success, and could be morally uplifting as well. The social programs of the 1930s passed through the warfare state to ultimately become the welfare state.

In the 1950s an emphasis on senior citizens, begun with the Social Security Act and set aside because of World War II, experienced resurgence. Programs to study seniors began, and gerontology started to develop as a field. More legislation was added to the books. Politically, seniors began to organize and put pressure on the system.

AT THE ZENITH OF THE WELFARE STATE

The culture became even more supportive of the disadvantaged and their plight in the 1960s. The revolutions of the 1960s were to some degree a natural extension of a release of this energy. Similarly, the poverty program represented structural affirmation that more needed to be done for the disadvantaged. The dark forces in our culture were, temporarily at least, at bay. The welfare state was on a roll. The 1960 period seems to be a high point in recent history, where there was a confluence of attitudes in support of and programs in support of the poor.

WHAT GOES UP OFTEN COMES DOWN

However, several interrelated events conspired to allow for the resurgence of older values and attitudes. Just as success in welfare programs and war making had stimulated support for government activity in the welfare area, failures in both those arenas—Vietnam and the War on Poverty—created a certain disillusionment within the cultural system concerning governmental activities in general and aid to the poor specifically. Hence, attitudes which were clearly present but somewhat less prominent began to return to prominence. Those attitudes can be clearly seen in the data here.

Overall, American society, because of its founding ethos, has, and will probably continue to have, hostility toward the disadvantaged, even given the cultural changes brought about by the Depression. The poorfare culture is strong and present, though its strength at any given moment may be greater or lesser than at any other moment. Poorfare culture focuses on the causes of poverty and makes judgments about them rather than the conditions of poverty and the problems poverty presents.

THE CORROSIVE CULTURE

Poorfare culture has two central features that act as corrosives to American society. Firstly, it overindividualizes the causes of poverty and thus periodically and regularly overindividualizes the mechanisms of relief. Economic reform, the provision of jobs, and the provision of training tend to be second rather than first-order activities.

Second, it overmoralizes the meaning of and the causes of poverty and thus infinitely complicates our ability to deal with the problem. Recognition of these two factors, overindividualization and overmoralization, will have to be central in welfare reform efforts in the future.

SOCIAL WORK IN THE POORFARE STATE

The difference between the welfare state and the poorfare state is the difference between what we do and what we think and feel. The poorfare state addresses the level of reluctance to provide benefits, the suspicion about the motives for program use which adheres to recipients, and the stigma which often characterizes social positions of poverty and older age. While American society is not totally poorfare in orientation, that perspective is certainly present, vigorous, and a dominant element for the social welfare system in general and the social work profession, in particular, to consider. It impacts the social work profession in several ways.

First, as a profession dedicated to helping those less advantaged in society, we need to understand more fully our culture's indecision and uncertainty about them. While it is often clear to us what programs are needed and what services ought to be provided, others in the system (legislators, administrators, the media) frequently disagree. Social workers are sometimes made to feel that their commitments are the result of an absence of toughness ("bleeding hearts") or an endorsement of dependency. A perspective which outlines the cultural and social structure of the ambivalence our society feels will be helpful.

Second, social workers and members of the social welfare professions will, doubtless, share some of these approach-avoidance orientations toward the poor and the older adult. Being a part of this society makes it impossible to escape. Societal uncertainties become our own as well; therefore, an understanding of the culture helps us toward an understanding of ourselves.

But comparisons between the poor and older citizens may help us do more than understand the contradictions which beset the helping professions. It may help the helpers design more effective intervention techniques. This point means more than "to be forewarned is to be forearmed," though that is certainly an important element. The social attention toward the poor and the old has had some different elements, involving support for the elderly through policy development while suspicion of the poor remained high. Despite Estes (1979) claim that policy toward the elderly leaves much undone, one can study the way in which aging policy has articulated, coped, and dealt with American value contradictions, and has done so with much success, as a model which can perhaps be adapted to other groups. In this case, understanding leads to positive action.

CONCLUSION

A welfare state can develop and flourish, then, in a poorfare culture because there are contradictory forces within that culture. Indeed, one might think of the welfare state as in part "counterphobic": We do more because we feel guilty about wanting to do less. Culture is not all of a piece. And there is more than guilt; there is fear. There is fear of them encroaching on us, fear of riots, and fear of facing demands for explanations of our own wealth we cannot answer.

There are also structural pressures. Other countries are doing it, and our politicians want to keep up with the Europeans. Big cataclysms—the Depression of the 1930s and World War II—caused fundamental changes in our willingness to help and our willingness to have the government help. Success was a positive reinforcement. Other cataclysms where failure was a leitmotif— Vietnam and the War on Poverty—allowed the resurgence of traditional and more negative values.

Part II

PICTURES IN PLENTY: CONCEPTIONS OF THE UNDERCLASS

The chapters in this section explore what people themselves think about the poor. The first chapters look at the public's views (in Boston and Kansas City) in response to an open-ended question: "Tell me about the lowest class and the next-to-the-lowest class." The use of a "lowest class" and "next-to-the-lowest class" framework gives respondents a chance to tell the interviewer how they, as respondents, defined the situation. It is then possible to pull together the responses into some kind of coherent picture of what the respondents did think about each group—and the thoughts were different.

This procedure has its perils; the categories constructed here have only "face" validity, and they need to be checked by other research. But they represent a start, an initial assay into the nature of the ideas people have about the poor. One positive thought is that we have the views of the lowest class themselves to put into play here.

A second study looks at the opinions of County Welfare Directors around the United States to see what they themselves think and what they believe the public thinks. Finally, data are provided for mothers of sixth-grade children in Detroit in the mid-1960s on their opinion of public and private agencies.

The overall picture is one of negativism toward the poor. The persistence of negative views of the poor during the height of programmatic expansion in just this area is interesting.

The degree of values persistence in the face of contrary action, or, alternatively, the degree to which we can act in ways contrary to values, or at least some variance with them, is impressive. It suggests two kinds of tensions. One is between and among values we all hold (Tropman 1989). It also suggests a values–action tension; conflicts between what we believe and think, on the one hand, and what we do on the other. Each may be used, or functions, in part at least, to control the other (see especially Tropman 1989).

Chapter 3

Laggards and Lushes: Images of the Poor

If the poverty programs, and the poor themselves, are surrounded by "constant crisis," if the poor are disliked (Klebaner 1964), and if they are the recipients of the stigma and hostility of many citizens (for a review, see Grosskind 1987; Himmelfarb 1983; Cameron 1975; Fallows 1982; Martin and Zald 1981), then it must be because the poor engage central values in the American social system. It is for this reason, perhaps, that the poor threaten the nonpoor, evoking concerns and fears for which stigma is a solution.

One way to empirically examine the validity of these ideas is to ask a sample of people a general descriptive question about the poor, and examine the responses. The words and phrases such respondents use to describe the "lowest class" should thus be indicative of stigma and "threat." Further, we would expect the population at large to base their view on the sense of "fate control" respondents felt was involved (Tropman and Strate 1983). For example, gender and race are not changeable. Illness and family crises are usually unpreventable, and old age ultimately affects everyone. Moral status, on the other hand, may be considered under the individual's control.

As people describe their feelings about the lowest classes, it seems that they are more likely to mention those items and characteristics which are alterable, like behavior, than those which the individual cannot control, like gender and race. Such an emphasis stresses the attribution of control to one's fate.

HOW THE STUDY WAS DONE

The study from which these data were taken (for this chapter and the next) is part of a large study of public attitudes on a variety of topics. The Joint Center for Urban Studies interviewed a cross section of people (N = 191) in Boston and Kansas City in 1971. One set of questions asked about class characteristics (class defined by respondent):

Now I have two final groups I want to ask you about: One group is often called "lower class but not the lowest" and another group is "people who are at the very bottom of the ladder." What differences would you see between these two groups? (Probes: How are they different in Living Standards? Housing? Types of Jobs? Income?)

Distinguishing between the lowest class and the next to the lowest class provides an opportunity for the respondent to express his or her feelings about the poor with a minimum of guidance and suggestion. Responses refer to what the respondents said in answer to the question.

I read each response as recorded by the interviewer carefully. For purposes of this analysis, the written record had to contain key words. To see, for example, how many of the respondents viewed the poor as being on welfare, then the word "welfare," or such synonyms as "relief," "dole," or "government help," were coded. Low education had to have specific wording to that effect, such as "they are the ones with no training" or "they do not have enough education," or the like. The responses were coded separately for "the lowest class" and "the next-to-the-lowest class." The basis for this allocation came from reading the response in relationship to the other responses. Respondents generally began with those "at the very bottom of the ladder" and worked their way up. The responses of these interviewees had much more the character of the lowest class. The responses of the twenty-two women and seven men who could not distinguish between lowest and next to lowest were included in the lowest-class category because the responses they did make were generally reflective of the lowest class.

The respondents were coded into class levels by sociologist Richard Coleman, who had already done groundbreaking work in status imagery (Coleman and Neugarten 1971). He used a combination of "Occupational status, educational background of husband and wife, present standard-of-living, future expectations (of the young) pre-retirement position (of the old), club memberships, church affiliation, ethnic identifications, neighborhood choice, and interviewer's description" (Coleman 1973) in dividing the 191 respondents within class positions. Though the original scheme had six classes, upper (UU) and lower upper (LU) were combined into a single upper (U) grouping, giving a total of five classes. Of the total sample, twelve (6.62%) were Black, eleven Black women (11% of women) and one Black man (a little more than 1% of men) (see Table 3.1).

Table 3.1

Basic Distribution of Respondents by Gender and Class Level, 191 Respondents, Boston and Kansas City, 1971

| | Social Classes | | | | | |
Gender	Upper	Upper Middle	Lower Middle	Upper Lower	Lower Lower	Total
Women	2	17	33	40	8	100
Men	2	23	34	30	2	91
Total	4	40	67	70	10	191
% Women	2.0%	17.0%	33.0%	40.0%	8.0%	100%
% Men	2.2%	25.3%	37.4%	32.9%	2.2%	100%

THE WELFARE POOR

Perhaps the characteristic most often mentioned about the lowest class is that they are the welfare class (see Table 3.2). Overall, 45 percent of the respondents identified the lowest class as welfare recipients, people for whom welfare payments account for a regular and significant proportion of income. There is little difference between men and women, overall, within classes, in this attribution. In the public mind, the lowest class and the welfare class are

Table 3.2

The Welfare Poor: Proportions of Respondents by Class and Gender Who Mention Receipt of Welfare as a Characteristic of Lowest Class Status (191 Respondents, Boston and Kansas City, 1971)

| | Social Classes | | | | | |
Gender	Upper	Upper Middle	Lower Middle	Upper Lower	Lower Lower	Total
Women	50.0%	58.0%	40.0%	35.0%	62.5%	43.0%
Men	50.0%	29.2%	50.0%	60.0%	50.0%	48.0%
Total	50.0%	41.4%	44.8%	45.7%	60.0%	45.0%

Note: Here and in subsequent tables the proportions are calculated on the basis of cell frequencies, as displayed in Table 3.1. Each table contains the total respondents who "mention" a relevant item. Respondents may (and did) mention more than one item.

merged into a single group, people who need help regularly and for whom welfare has become a way of life. (There are some gender differences within classes, but these should not be overstressed because of small numbers.)

This perceived regularity of dependency is a significant one when compared with some national statistics of the period. In 1960, 17.8 percent of the poor were receiving welfare. By 1970, this coverage had risen to 46 percent nationally; yet, even with this 158-percent increase, more than half the poor were not receiving assistance. The most popular welfare program, the AFDC program, had even lower proportions: 8.2 percent and 32.9 percent for 1960 and 1970, respectively (Tropman 1974). These figures do not justify characterizing entire classes of people as the welfare poor.[1]

A straightforward interpretation of these results would seem to be that status stigma is one of the social mechanisms society uses to control welfare use. Indeed, one drops a whole class level by becoming a welfare recipient (see Chapter 4). Perhaps the most striking difference between the two lowest classes was the sense that the lowest class was the welfare class, while the next-to-the-lowest class were still working and struggling (see Chapter 4). In this impressionistic assessment, welfare takes on a broader meaning than program enrollment; rather, it indicates the difference between those who have given up and those who are still working, between the worthy poor and the unworthy poor.

THE UNTRAINED/UNSCHOOLED POOR

A second item which was frequently associated with the lowest class was a lack of education (see Table 3.3); 43.8 percent of the respondents mentioned this characteristic. Overall, 44 percent of the respondents mentioned inadequate education as characteristic of being in the lowest class. Modest variation was found by class, except in the upper class, where fewer respondents (25%) made this association. Somewhat more variation was found by gender.

Throughout America's history, and especially within recent times, getting an education has been thought of as the necessary and often sufficient condition for getting ahead (Miller and Roby 1970, 120). Education has the purpose not of developing intellectuals, but of opening channels for mobility. Hence, it is a symbol of mobility potential. The assertion that the lowest class is uneducated reaffirms this mythology.

Again, facts offer a different perspective. The relationship between education and later social status has stirred much controversy (Morgan 1962; Blau and Duncan 1967; Hodge and Treiman 1968; Schiller 1973; Jencks 1972). While the poor do have less education than the nonpoor, the parallels are far from perfect, especially for minority groups (Schiller 1973, 101; Duncan 1968, 90). This raises questions about how effective education is as a mobility mechanism when factors like discrimination are operating. Indeed, the extent to which the the poor are disproportionately people of color and women may be

Table 3.3
The Unschooled Poor: Proportions of Respondents by Class and Gender Who Mentioned Inadequate Education as a Cause of Lowest-Class Status (191 Respondents, Boston and Kansas City, 1971)

Gender		Social Classes				
	Upper	Upper Middle	Lower Middle	Upper Lower	Lower Lower	Total
Women	50.0%	35.0%	66.7%	25.0%	25.0%	41.0%
Men	—	37.0%	50.0%	46.7%	100.0%	46.0%
Total	25.0%	36.9%	58.1%	34.3%	50.0%	43.8%

due in part to the fact that these groups do not get the rewards for their education that society thinks generally is the case. While clearly important, education neither guarantees success nor prevents failure.

Dr. Richard Coleman (1973) notes that the poor are incorrectly seen as all having low education, while the rich are incorrectly seen as all having high education. In other words, the popular impression is that wealthy people have many advanced degrees, while poor people have very little schooling. The Morgan data (1962, 208) indicate the poor (less than $5,000 in 1959) have 31 percent less education than all families. Yet a substantial 19 percent of poor families' heads had twelve grades or more of education. On a correlation basis, Hodge and Treiman (1968, 724) found 0.2695 and 0.3049 for men and women, respectively, between family income and respondents' education, and they report a correlation of 0.5629 between occupation and respondents' education and occupation which is similar to Blau and Duncan's (1967, 169) finding of a 0.596 relationship between respondents' education and job in 1962. Nam, Powers, and Glick (1964, 19) reported on status crystallization that, in 1960, 9.4 percent of the low-status population (scores of 0–19, overall) had inconsistently high education, and 25.1 percent had inconsistently high occupation.

Yet education is the one thing which, according to popular belief, is within everyone's grasp (Miller and Roby 1970). Lack of schooling limits opportunities and at the same time limits income potential, an extension of the mobility theory. Implicit in this is the reverse statement; with education and training, the lowest class can achieve higher status and income.

It is worth noting that among middle-class respondents the proportion of men who ascribe lowest-class status in part to inadequate education is little different from the proportion of women. In the lower classes, however, men are much more likely than women to mention education. And in the upper class, men do not mention education as relevant. Thus, the lowest-class males regard education as a key to getting ahead, while those who have achieved high status feel it is barely necessary. Perhaps research into the social origins of upper-class men would reveal that attributes other than education are important (Baltzell 1964).

While education and getting ahead were the most popular words in these data, respondents also made specific references to mobility. One lower-middle-class male commented that the difference between the lowest class and the next-to-the-lowest class lay in the fact that the latter, "still have strong ideas of rising on the economic ladder," while the former, "don't care to try to rise." Other respondents mentioned "a lack of vertical mobility," "a lack of social skills," or "low aspirations" as characteristic of the lowest class.

THE DISTINGUISHABLE POOR

The poor threaten the general population by reminding them that they too could be poor. Class consciousness, the ability to distinguish between the lowest class and the next-to-the-lowest class is one measure of status perception (others are discussed in Chapter 4). By reminding respondents of status loss possibilities, the poor become a status threat. Threats are things people notice. If the poor represented no status threat, one would expect the survey respondents to have more trouble identifying them. In the presence of a threat, however, one tends to make distinctions to separate oneself from them. The proportion of respondents who could not distinguish between the lowest class and the next to the lowest class included 8 percent of the men and 22 percent of the women (see Table 3.4).

What is significant here is the numbers who did make the distinction: 78 percent of the women and 92 percent of the men. Men seem to be more threat-

Table 3.4
The Distinguishable Poor: Proportions of Respondents by Class and Gender Who Did Not or Could Not Make the Distinction between the Lowest and Next-to-the-Lowest Classes (191 Respondents, Boston and Kansas City, 1971)

Gender	Social Classes					
	Upper	Upper Middle	Lower Middle	Upper Lower	Lower Lower	Total
Women	50.0%	23.0%	15.0%	27.5%	12.0%	22.0%
Men	0	12.0%	2.9%	16.0%	50.0%	7.7%
Total	50.0%	17.0%	9.0%	19.0%	10.0%	15.0%

ened by the poor than women, except men already at the lower-lower position. As the chief perceived "carriers" of status, one would expect men to be more threatened. Further, lower-lower-class men would have a reason not to make this distinction. They would only be identifying themselves. Women, on the other hand, might not be as status conscious or might use other status measures not mentioned or noticed here. For example, women, knowing that returns to education are not, for women, what they are for men, might not pay as much attention to salary, income, and money.

This observation is supported by another. Professions dealing with the threatening poor, especially social work, are heavily populated with women. This situation may obtain because in the past women had derived status from the man with whom they were associated—their fathers and then their husbands—rather than from a job or from their associates. I want to emphasize I am reflecting a practice, not endorsing it. Over the years, the recruitment to the social work profession has tended to represent women from middle-class backgrounds and men from working-class backgrounds (Gockle 1966). In the past, a woman could associate with lower-status people without feeling the risk of status loss that men might have felt.

For both men and women, the middle class seems to contain significant polarities, with the lower middle being most sensitive (fewest who could not distinguish) to class consciousness, and the upper middle being least sensitive. This finding deserves further consideration and research, especially because of the small numbers involved in this survey. It may be that the transition from lower middle to upper middle is a crucial one.

THE NONWORKING POOR

One of the strongest images we have of the poor is that somehow it is their "fault" that they are poor. This view is implicit in the tradition of individualism so prominent in Western culture, which holds that each person is responsible for his or her fate. The central thesis is that the poor are poor because they do not work and do not want to work. In the simplest sense, lack of work results in lack of income, which is synonymous with poverty. The definition extends to poverty of character, because to not work is, within the traditions of Calvin, Marx, and Weber, to have no sense of worth. Poor thus means poor in spirit and poor in moral stature, as well as poor in income (see Table 3.5). About 28.7 percent of the respondents mention something about problems of employment in connection with the lowest class. This proportion, though not insubstantial, is not as large as the proportion who felt the poor were the welfare class, nor the proportion who thought them to be educationally deprived. And again, there is a definite difference between the responses of men and women. Men, almost 34 percent of them, mention work-related items as characteristics of the lowest class, while only 24 percent of the women mention this element. It is also interesting to note that it is the men and women in

Table 3.5
The Nonworking Poor: Proportions of Respondents by Class and Gender Who Mentioned Work Problems as a Cause of Lowest-Class Status (191 Respondents, Boston and Kansas City, 1971)

| | Social Classes | | | | | |
Gender	Upper	Upper Middle	Lower Middle	Upper Lower	Lower Lower	Total
Women	50.0%	29.4%	18.2%	27.5%	12.5%	24.0%
Men	100.0%	45.8%	29.4%	26.7%	—	33.7%
Total	75.0%	39.0%	23.9%	27.1%	10.0%	28.7%

the upper and upper-middle classes who are most likely to mention work-related problems in connection with the lowest class. Indeed, there is a general inverse relationship between class level and the mention of work. None of the men of the lower class, but all of the men of the upper class, mentioned work.[2]

THE FAULT-FILLED POOR

Work may be a sort of general catch-all target for many kinds of blame. Because of its importance, mentions of "fault" and "not their fault" for lowest-class status were coded directly (see Table 3.6). Of the respondents, 34 percent made some comment indicating it was the poor's fault they were poor, often stated in terms of laziness, lack of motivation, or lack of ambition. Only 10 percent of the respondents made some comment indicating that the position of lowest status was not the fault of the person in it. They mentioned lack of jobs, discrimination, poor opportunities, and the like. In 75 percent of comparisons, men were somewhat more likely than women to assign personal responsibility, and the tone of the more common responses was hostile—with a blaming character—as well as faultfinding.

Overall, the respondents were much more likely to attribute lowest-class status to failings within the person instead of within the system. As will be suggested later, this line of thinking protects the integrity of the middle class or nonpoor person's thinking about his or her own status, since it implicitly requires that one's fortune is under one's own control. I would expect the reverse of this approach to obtain if we asked people to evaluate the highest class and the next to the highest class. In that event, and for similar reasons, we would expect that people would see highest-class status based heavily upon external, impersonal conditions. This line of thinking works out well

Table 3.6
The Fault-Filled Poor: Moralism—Proportions of Respondents by Class and Gender Who Ascribe Fault or No-Fault to the Lowest Class (191 Respondents, Boston and Kansas City, 1971)

Gender		Social Classes				
	Upper	Upper Middle	Lower Middle	Upper Lower	Lower Lower	Total
"Their Fault"						
Women	—	35.3%	27.3%	32.5%	25.0%	30.0%
Men	—	16.7%	47.1%	46.7%	50.0%	33.0%
Total	—	24.4%	37.3%	38.6%	30.0%	33.9%
"Not Their Fault"						
Women	50.0%	11.8%	6.1%	7.5%	12.5%	9.0%
Men	—	16.7%	8.7%	13.3%	—	12.0%
Total	25.0%	14.6%	7.5%	10.0%	10.0%	10.0%

for the thinker, whatever his or her status. Those below are there because of their fault, and, "I will not do those things and hence that will not happen to me, while those above are there because of luck and chance, and thus I cannot be faulted for not being there instead of where I am. It is just luck!"

All classes seemed concerned with making some comment on this issue. Males, especially in the lower middle and lower classes, had very high proportions of faultfinding statements, suggesting one source of hostility to the poor. Indeed the closer one is to a problematic status, the more one might wish to separate oneself from it. It is worth noting that a variable Feagin (1972) used, luck and chance, did not appear here at all. He used a threefold categorization to describe explanations for poverty: individualistic (your fault), structural (the system's fault), and fatalistic (luck and chance). Of course, what people say and what they think are of course not always the same, but there is a strong pattern here.

THE INDIVIDUAL POOR

In analyses of answers, what is not mentioned is perhaps as significant as what is mentioned. Certain factors often statistically associated with lowest-class status, as represented by poverty-inducing conditions, were surprising by their absence. Age, family disorganization, and illness were among the more obvious omissions (see Table 3.7). Only 2 percent of the respondents

Table 3.7
The Individual Poor: Individualism—Proportion of Respondents by Class and Gender Who Saw Age, Family Disorganization, or Illness as Causes of Poverty (191 Respondents, Boston and Kansas City, 1971)

		Social Classes				
Gender	Upper	Upper Middle	Lower Middle	Upper Lower	Lower Lower	Total
Women	0	29.4%	24.2%	7.5%	50.0%	20.0%
Men	50.0%	12.5%	14.7%	6.6%	50.0%	13.0%
Total	25.0%	19.5%	19.4%	7.1%	50.0%	16.7%

mention age, and 4.2 percent mention family disorganization. About 17 percent mention illness, so the illness data are fully displayed.

Aging has been associated with poverty since the passage of the Social Security Act, at the very least. Family disorganization has also been a popular topic of discussion with respect to the status of poverty. And illness, of course, as it can interrupt a steady income, is an important associate, if not a cause, of poverty. Yet these do not receive strong notice at all.

Perhaps one reason is precisely because their denial is inverse to the centrality of individualism in American life. American society is individualistically oriented, prizing inner direction over other direction (Reisman, Glazer, and Denney 1956). Age, family disorganization, and illness are indeed important, but represent areas in which others (people or conditions) must play a role in causing status decline and helping us through or with it. Yet respondents may not feel they control these elements, and thus a certain amount of denial may occur. A lack of willingness to vocalize these dimensions may be present, not because they are unimportant, but because they reflect unacceptable value emphasis and a recognition that some causal elements of status may, indeed, be beyond our control.

THE ASCRIPTIVE POOR

A look at ascriptive statuses might prove of interest. These are caste-like social positions which are hard to change. Female status, immigrant status, and racial status are likely candidates for lowest-class associations. However, it did not happen.

Proportions of persons who mentioned women and/or immigrants as status designations characterizing the lowest class were identical at 1.04 percent. Ethnicity was mentioned by 5.2 percent (see Table 3.8). This result is doubly

Table 3.8
The Ascriptive Poor: Individualism—Proportion of Respondents by Class and Gender Who Mentioned Women, Race, or Immigrant Status, as a Cause of Lowest Status (191 Respondents, Boston and Kansas City, 1971)

Gender	Social Classes					
	Upper	Upper Middle	Lower Middle	Upper Lower	Lower Lower	Total
Women	—	5.9%	3.0%	—	—	2.0%
Men	—	25.0%	2.9%	3.3%	—	8.7%
Total	—	17.0%	3.0%	1.4%	—	5.2%

surprising since the welfare category which has received the most adverse publicity—the AFDC program—is for women and children. Hence, there is some inconsistency in these responses unless one wishes to assume that respondents felt they had already mentioned women by virtue of mentioning welfare.

Perhaps most surprising and provocative of all is the low proportion, 5.2 percent, of people who identified race as a characteristic of the lowest class. This result confounds those who see class prejudices as a cover for race prejudice. At least insofar as these data were concerned, the two appear to be quite separate. However, the time period of the 1960s may have made vocalizing race prejudice not politically correct. And it is not the case that people were feeling sympathetic toward the lowest class—recall that 34 percent of those surveyed accused the members of the lowest class of fault for their social status. Rather, it seems that the general public is making a distinction between class and race.

There are interesting patterns by sex and class in racial attributions. Overall, men in greater proportions than women consider race as a factor in lowest-class status. Notably, the upper-middle classes again have the highest proportions of male and female persons who see race as a factor in lowest-class status. The upper-middle-class male has, for this distribution, a very high proportion of respondents, 25 percent, who think this way. So while the rest of their compeers are separating class and race, this group is more likely to fuse the two.

SUBDOMINANCE OF THE POOR

So far the emphasis has been placed on the responses item by item, dimension by dimension. The last set of considerations deals with an attempt to characterize the overall responses in some pattern or shape. Two features stand out. The first is the extent to which the respondents linked the poor and lowest class to subdominant rather than dominant American values. The second is a consideration of the order in which mentions emerged from the responses.

In several previous works (summarized in Tropman 1989), a set of value dimensions crucial to American society was introduced. These dimensions are as follows: independence, mobility, status, work, moralism, individualism, and ascription.[3] Within each dimension there are competing, contesting elements or ways of achieving the value-goal in question (see Chapter 1). These conflicts are as follows:

1. Independence   Self-reliance versus interdependency
2. Mobility   Contest versus sponsored modes
3. Status   Achievement versus equality
4. Work   Career versus job
5. Moralism   Freedom versus control individualism
6. Individualism   Inner versus other direction
7. Ascription   Performance versus quality distinctions

The argument advanced from a values-conflict perspective is one which suggests that within key values dimensions are conflicting values, pairs or sets of competing commitments which conflict with each other. Self-reliance versus interdependency refers to the extent one achieves independence through relying on self alone or through networks of others in exchange. Contest mobility refers to earning of status, while sponsorship refers to nonmerit connections, like family ones. Career orientation reflects one's view of work as involving increasing responsibility and reward; job orientation refers to completing the specific task at hand. Achievement orientation reflects difference and self-aggrandizement; equality refers to status bases to which all citizens have similar access, regardless of personal differences. Freedom refers to lack of constraint as a prime commitment; control refers to the necessity of direction (policy, law, etc.) as a crucial commitment. Inner direction highlights one's own judgment as a source of guidance; other direction emphasizes the importance of those around us as guides. Performance criteria reflect the view, "If one can do the job, one has the job." Qualitative criteria, like being a certain race or gender, "interrupt" performance judgments. The argument reflected here is that the dominant values are those on the left in each pair, the subdominant ones are those on the right. It was felt that the old and the poor would be more likely associated with subdominant values.

These relationships, of course, are far from perfect, but do suggest that the lowest class is associated with the absence of dominant orientations and the presence of subdominant ones.

The emphasis on welfare as a characteristic of the lowest class suggests a lack of self-reliance and a dependence on the government. The association of lack of education (43.8% mentioned this) with the lowest class implies an absence from the contest system of mobility that education requires. The importance of achievement was underscored by the few respondents who were not able to make the distinction between the two classes. Achievement orientation, of course, thrives on distinctions.

Equality was emphasized more by the women than the men, with 22 percent of the women making no distinction between the lowest and the next-to-lowest class. Men, however, seemed to be less egalitarian in this direction, and all but a small proportion of them (7.7%) appear class conscious.

Job orientation is the extent to which there is a lack of interest and advancement in work. The emphasis in these data on lack of work as a cause of lowest-class status (28.7% mentioned) is not as great as one might have thought. Perhaps the respondents felt the lowest class could not fit in even on the first rung of the job ladder, and would have to rely on welfare.

Control, of course, is clearly revealed in the extent to which the poor are seen as being in a condition which is their fault. The concept of fault is one which embodies and requires control. If the poor are avoiding responsibility, someone else, and perhaps the government, will have to step in.

Freedom and control exist together, and the lack of control at the personal level often means that controls are needed at higher, less desirable levels.

In the case of the first five values, it appears that the respondents could be thought of as mentioning the subdominant values, though job orientation is somewhat unclear. For the remaining two, individualism and ascription, the pattern is unclear, because of the few references made to them. The last two values were not stressed, and therefore may be set aside for our purposes.

HIERARCHY OF MENTIONS/ASSOCIATIONS

It has been noted that the respondents not only mentioned key value dimensions, but also tended to emphasize the subdominant side of those dimensions. An additional factor is worth noting. These comments were often inversely related to the perceived changeability or controllability of the dimensions—welfare, education, and work—receiving the most mentions. These items can change fairly quickly. These were followed followed by age, family disorganization, and illness. These are tougher to change. Last, and almost impossible to change, were gender, ethnicity, and race. This ordering describes the data (see Table 3.9). The point here is that, when describing what characterizes lowest-class status, Americans like, it seems, to emphasize things that are controllable and changeable over those things which are not. That gives everyone hope.

Independence is first, in frequency of mentions, followed by mobility, status, work, and moral value perceptions. All of these elements can be regarded

Table 3.9
A Hierarchy of Associations with "Lowest Class"

	Value	Indicator	% Women	% Men	Total	(Table)
			Response			
1.	Independence	Welfare	43%	48%	45%	(3.2)
2.	Mobility	Education	41%	46%	44%	(3.3)
3.	Status	Distinguish between Lowest Class and Next-to-Lowest Class	28%	7%	15%	(3.4)
4.	Work	Work	24%	34%	29%	(3.5)
5.	Moral	Fault				
	Their Fault		30%	38%	34%	(3.6)
	Not Their Fault		9%	12%	10%	
6.	Individualism					
	Age		—	—	2%	
	Family Disorganization		—	—	4%	(3.7)
	Illness		20%	13%	17%	
7.	Ascription					
	Sex		—	—	1%	
	Ethnicity		—	—	1%	(3.8)
	Race		2%	9%	5%	

as changeable and under the control of the individual. Individualism and as-cription followed (with mentions of lowest status and [older] age as a proxy).

Several points should be made about this hierarchy. First, while the rank-ing differs whether one views the responses of men, women, or both groups together, independence is clearly first and mobility second. Second, within this framework those responses which signify the possibility of change or control appear first in the list, while those which imply inevitability appear last. (A similar type of ranking was found in a multiyear study of policy values; see Tropman and Strate 1983.)

IMAGE OF THE POOR

These perceptions suggest that time can be well spent in thinking about the intellectual and emotional structures of views about the poor, especially since the poor (the upper-lower and lower-lower groups) seem as negative about themselves as everyone else.

Basically, it seems that the poor must be thought of and discussed in terms that will not challenge the integrity of the achievements of the nonpoor or suggest that their current status might be subject to forces outside of their control. For example, if a middle-class person argues that luck and chance play a significant role in the status of the poor person, then that person should allow that luck and chance influenced his or her own career. This admission tends to belittle their achievement, and implies that their own future position might well be dependent on things beyond their control. Similarly, if a nonpoor person argues that the system is an important cause of a citizen being in the lowest class, then he or she is, at the same time, acknowledging his or her own dependence on the system. The uncontrollability of fate as opposed to the potential comprehension of and control of individual or structural features might explain in part why our respondents did not mention fateful events as characteristic of the lowest class. Calling an event fateful removes it from the realm of potential control.

But why, one might ask, should it matter very much whether one's status is due to personal effort or external conditions? Two assumptions are involved here, central to the personal nature of achievement and the ideology of personal control of one's fate. The first is that if external status is an indicator of internal quality, then somehow "fairness" and "justice" demand that the external be proportional to the internal. Hence, pride in status reflects a deeper pride in self. Climbing the status ladder is climbing the ladder of personal worth.

An evaluative problem of serious proportions develops when one's social status or fiscal status is clearly a result of ill-gotten gains, or when there is an incontestable discrepancy between one's fiscal position and one's moral position, as in the case of some members of organized crime. Crime, in Bell's (1960) phrase, has become "a queer ladder of social mobility," and remains one of the curious contradictory conundrums of American society.

Any suggestion that status is due to forces other than personal effort threatens the link between moral status and social status, and will tend to be rejected. The illusion of personal control is important, in that one cannot be fairly and justly evaluated on the status outcome if one did not control the important variables from which status is derived. Hence, despite the problems of unemployment, we cling to the mythology that work, and especially hard work, will lead to success.

The second assumption refers to our sense of control. If status is due to external factors solely, or even heavily, then whatever achievements we enjoy are not only temporary and not due to us (bad enough), but may be taken from us in a moment (even worse).

Thus, the link between moral status and social status and the illusion of personal control become implicated in our perceptions of the poor. If poor people were not morally at fault, then one would have to ask uncomfortable questions about himself or herself; if poor people did not have control over their lives, then one would need to question the amount of control a nonpoor person has over his or her own life.

There are two further aspects to the comfort which the nonpoor derive from their views of the poor beyond simple support of the status quo. They are concerned about the possibility that (1) they might someday be poor, and (2) what might happen if they were. Point 1 is served by the previous argument: Since poverty is related to moral failing, the absence of such a failing (by virtue of being in higher-class status) is solace. Furthermore, since poverty is within the control of the poor person, it is presumably also within the control of the nonpoor person, who has thus far been able to avoid it.

But what if one does, by some quirk of fate, become poor? The structure of the images of the poor serve here. It is recalled that the poor were seen as characterized by those things which they could change, rather than by ascriptive characteristics. The nonpoor person is thus further assured against becoming poor and comforted to be convinced that poverty has an exit. These are the functions of the nonpoor person's explanations for the existence of poverty. One further implication here is that the reverse of this argument is likely to apply. Fault is important for explaining status up to one's own status level for the same reason, luck and chance are important in explaining status above that of the particular respondent. (Recall the comment about one's views about the explanation for those of status below you [their fault] and those above you [luck].)

In sum, this line of thinking removes, for most Americans, the need to be too concerned about the poor person, something Heilbroner (1970) has referred to as a lack of social magnanimity. It defines the poor person in such a way as to not only remove worth, but to prevent erosion of one's own self-esteem and to actually enhance that self-esteem.

It is hard to overstress the point that defining the plight of the poor as a response to personalistic control elements not only fails to erode one's own achievements, but also enhances them, since it gives credit to the decisions made by the individual in question and provides a person about whom he or she need not feel bad, and whom he or she can be "better than." One may be better than the old, blind, and disabled, or the Blacks or women, but somehow it is known that the competition was not fair. Hence, being better does not provide the internalized feeling or gratification and sanctity that being better than someone else in a fair fight would. Indeed, it may actually enhance guilt. To fully enjoy one's gains, one must also feel that one deserves them.

POLICY IMPLICATIONS

This line of thinking has some social policy implications worthy of mention. First, if indeed the poor are threatening, then bringing them to the attention of the public will only bring about further rejection. It is necessary to find ways of calling the attention of the public at large to this problem without making arguments and explanations which will reinforce the status anxieties of the middle American.

Related to this is the second possibility, one of educating the public about the poor. The problem is not middle-class misperceptions about the poor, implying, as that does, that education with the facts will help. That solution ignores the psychological energy and needs behind views of the poor. The argument here is that the conceptions have much more to do with the concerns of all classes for themselves and are not, in any specific sense, directed only at the poor. The poor themselves have misconceptions about the poor. We thus need to make new attempts to provide facts that may change the images in people's minds.

Third, these results suggest a set of problems for professions which systematically deal with the poor, especially social work. Specifically, there is not much support, in these responses, for pleas for support of the poor due to the external nature of the causes of poverty. And unlike education, which is connected with the myths of upward mobility, social work can draw strength from no deep reservoir of values. Perhaps it could seek in some way to connect itself with mobility and achievement values as a way to enhance its ability to be helpful.

Fourth, it is now clear from the responses that the middle class is one important source of hostility to welfare programs. Those involved in designing new programs to help those in the lowest class will need to think of ways to avoid the stigma attached to many current programs, stigma which comes from a sense that the lowest-class members have a heavy hand of responsibility in their own fate.

The important point here, however, is to see that the problems are centrally, not peripherally, related to key American values, and it is therefore necessary to take those values into account in both analysis and policy.

CONCLUSION

The old explanation, which points out that "support of an ideology is strongest among those who profit most from the system which the ideology explains" (Rytina, Form, and Pease 1970, 715), still rings true. The question remains, however, as to who profits from certain ideologies about the poor. As Pogo, the comic strip possum created by Walt Kelly, famously said, "We have met the enemy, and he is us."

NOTES

1. Williamson (1974b) found similar inaccuracies, except for the proportion of illegitimates, in people's perceptions of the welfare clientele.

2. The relationship between class and work ethic was studied by Williamson (1974a). He found almost no relationship between class level and this specific variable. However, education related negatively to work. Obviously, more research is needed here.

3. Most of these dimensions are self-explanatory, but a word here would not be out of place. Independence refers to the desire for freedom, reliance upon one's own resources, and ability to avoid constraints. Being on welfare is such a constraint. Mobility captures the desire to get ahead in society, to move up the ladder and avoid moving down. Education is an important indicator of the mobility value because it suggests a desire to get ahead. Status refers to the basis (ascribed or achieved, for example) for the positions one holds. Respondents being able to distinguish between the lowest and the next-to-the-lowest class is one kind of measure of status. Work alerts us to the crucial nature of contribution to the society over time, and reaping the rewards that attend such a contribution. Seeing lack of work as a cause of lowest-class status is an important measure of status. Moralism points to American's tendency to make judgments about the world and the people in it. Fault orientation assesses this dimension. Individualism reflects an emphasis on the self and its importance. As noted, dimensions such as older age, family disorganization, and illness, which tend to point up our dependence on others, are problematic in an independence-oriented society. Finally, ascription, which brings to the fore American tendencies to look at involuntary categories as a basis for judgment—categories like gender, race, and ethnic status—is important to consider.

Chapter 4

The Decent Poverty Stricken:
Images of the Near Poor

The status poor—those at the bottom of the ladder—are a threatening group to the citizens of the poorfare state because of the possibilities they embody and imply. Even thinking about the poor must be done cautiously, such that one does not inadvertently devalue one's own achievements and merits or one's image of those accomplishments. What happens, though, when one changes from thinking about the bottom class to the next rung? How do people think about the next-to-the-lowest class?

The members are seen as decent poverty-stricken individuals. If the lowest class can be regarded as the welfare class, the class which has given up, then the next-lowest class is perceived as one which has continued to try and is still interested in achieving success, or has, above all, the motivation, the will, or the nerve to try. Respondents see these class members as continuing to struggle to control the elements of their lives (rather than abandoning themselves to the vicissitudes of the environment). Indeed, several respondents specifically described members of this group as people who did have some control over their own life, or words to that effect. The beliefs about the next-lowest class, like the lowest class, support and enhance major value systems. Rather than threatening values, like the lowest class, the near-poor provide reassurance of the dominant values. While the poor threaten values, near-poor provide reassurance. In a sense, if the poor represent the most subdominant elements of the value system, the near-poor represent the dominant ones.

DATA AND APPROACH

The same data used in the previous chapter are used here; however, in analyzing the findings for the next-to-the-lowest class, it became apparent that some additional specifications were necessary to handle the responses. Whereas in the lowest class, "welfare" had been the key response word, the view toward the next-to-the-lowest class included additional response motifs using less harsh phrases like "government subsidy," "government help," and so on.

In addition, there were many mentions of "trying" or "effort" in relation to maintaining independence. Thus a category for effort was included. Furthermore, most of the mentions of welfare specifically for this class were in the context of occasional need, or the mixture of welfare with work, a temporary allotment to "make ends meet."

For the lowest class, education deficit had been used as a key indicator of mobility (see Table 3.3). In referring to the next-to-the-lowest class, however, there were broader mentions of "getting ahead," as distinct from just "education." A code was added for these. People said specifically that this class "still hopes to get ahead" or "wants to rise." Twelve men (14%) and five women (6%) made such a reference. Of course, "get ahead of whom?" is a question. Usual answers to this question include others, one's family, one's father, or one's earlier self, among other possibilities.

The greatest shift came in the enhancement of the status variable. With respect to the lowest class, class consciousness had become the key measure, operationalized by whether or not the respondent had, in fact, made a distinction between the lowest class and the next-to-the-lowest class (see Table 3.4). In looking at the next-to-the-lowest class, however, that distinction was insufficient. In addition, attention is now paid not only to class consciousness, but what it was that people were class conscious about.

Three factors became important: the nature of the occupation, the nature and style of housing or neighborhood (see Hollingshead and Redlich 1958), and, perhaps not surprisingly, the lifestyle of the class (Coleman and Neugarten 1971; Warner 1949), as indicated by vacations, luxuries, and the like. Twenty-eight women (35%) mentioned this last factor, with many of them specifically mentioning the lack of vacations or recreation as a class characteristic.

These variables might be considered status as opposed to mobility variables. Mobility means ability to get ahead; status means a sensitivity to class distinctions, a sensitivity which hinges on the nature of the work, housing, and lifestyle of the person. These respondents spontaneously suggested these distinctions. All, of course, imply the process of evaluation of others (assessment, judging) which Zeldich stresses (1968, 255). However, they were also often mentioned with respect to the lowest class, and, in many other instances, a comparison seemed to be implicit. For example, if a respondent mentioned that the next-to-the-lowest class had "better housing," one might expect he or she meant "than the lowest class," even though the latter group has not been specifically mentioned.

For purposes of contrast, therefore, the lowest-class data were reanalyzed with attention to these new categories. Of these analyses, "government aid," (independence) and "mobility" were negligible factors in the comments about the lowest class and are not reported. The extent of effort (or the absence or lack of effort) was perceived in the lowest class as a negative characteristic. Many of the respondents mentioned that the lowest class "didn't try" anymore, and no one mentioned it with respect to the next-to-the-lowest class.

Among the status variables, the respondents mentioned jobs, housing, and impaired lifestyle in reference to the lowest class. Of those three, only housing was mentioned with very much frequency with respect to the next-to-the-lowest class.

As before, the data were read response by response, and specific mentions of the categories were noted. The number of respondents differs from those in Chapter 3 because all of the respondents did not mention the lowest class and the next-to-the-lowest class. Twenty-two women and seven men did not make that distinction; however, of that group, seven women and two men made a reference sufficiently explicit so that their responses could be used (see Table 4.1).

AN IMPORTANT SHIFT

The responses generally represent a shift in orientation and attitude from those found characterizing lowest class. Overall, one has the impression of a positive, not negative, attitude toward the second-lowest class. The responses reflect grudging admiration for people who are seen as independent, resourceful, and determined to get ahead, but who have had problems and difficulties which do not seem to be their fault.

INDEPENDENCE: THE TRYING POOR SUPPLEMENT (THE WELFARE POOR SUPPLANT)

The nature of the responses here is different from those made in reference to the lowest class (see Table 4.2A). In general, welfare is mentioned much less often: Only 9 percent of the respondents cited welfare as a characteristic of the second-lowest class. The actual wording of the answers suggests the belief that people go on and off welfare, using it for occasional, not total, support. This shift is represented clearly as the wording softens from "welfare" to phrases like "government aid," "charity," and so on (see Table 4.2B).

The second-lowest class is seen as trying. Approximately 21 percent of the respondents indicated that the second-lowest class was seen as putting forth effort and trying to achieve success, but there was a great variation by class (see Table 4.2C), though mostly between lower-lower and other classes.

Table 4.1
Answered Questions by Class and Race

		Class Levels				
	Upper	Upper Middle	Lower Middle	Upper Lower	Lower Lower	Total
Females						
Grand Total	2	17	33	40	8	100
Those Who Did Make Distinction	1	13	28	29	7	78
Those Who Did Not Make Distinction	1	4	5	11	1	22
Working Total[a]	1	15	28	31	7	82
Males						
Grand Total	2	23	34	30	2	91[b]
Those Who Did Make Distinction	2	20	33	28	1	85
Those Who Did Not Make Distinction	0	3	1	2	1	7
Working Total[c]	2	21	33	29	2	87
Grand Working Total	36	61	60	9	169	—

[a]Twenty-two women did not make the distinction between lowest class and next-to-the-lowest class. Of these twenty-two, seven people spoke of the next-to-the-lowest class, or referred directly to it, permitting use of their response and giving a working total of eighty-two.

[b]Between the initial analysis and the current one, 1 upper middle-class male card was lost. Thus, our total here is one less than in Chapter 3.

[c]Seven of the men did not make the distinction between lowest class and next-to-the-lowest class. Of the seven, two spoke of the next-to-the-lowest class, or referred directly to it, permitting use of their responses and giving a working total of eighty-seven.

The shift in language reflects a shift in the belief about what is happening within the second-lowest class, as they are perceived by respondents. One still tries his or her best, but one also needs external supports occasionally. These concessions are approved and even applauded, as long as they are accompanied by effort. It is only when the effort becomes supplanted (rather than supplemented) by help of a constant sort that the respondents lose sympathy.

While there are only some mildly strong class differences, there is a sustained gender difference which deserves mention. Females are more likely to mention interdependence than men, with respect to the next-to-the-lowest

Table 4.2
Independence: Proportions of Respondents by Class and Gender Who Mention Welfare, Government Aid, and Effort as Characteristic of the Second-Lowest Class (169 Respondents, Boston and Kansas City, 1971)

		Social Class				
	Upper	Upper Middle	Lower Middle	Upper Lower	Lower Lower	Total
A: Use of Welfare						
Women	50%	20%	11%	10%	—	12%
Men	—	5%	—	14%	—	6%
Total	33%	11%	5%	12%	—	9%
B: Government Aid						
Women	—	46%	32%	22%	57%	33%
Men	—	5%	6%	14%	—	8%
Total	—	22%	18%	18%	44%	20%
C: Are Trying						
Women	—	33%	21%	29%	74%	26%
Men	—	5%	24%	21%	—	17%
Total	—	16%	23%	26%	11%	21%

class. It may be that women are more sensitive to the problems involved in "making ends meet" than men, or perhaps they may be more sensitive to the dependencies involved in accepting welfare. In others words, women could be more sensitive than men to the importance of external dependence, or, more precisely, the mix of dependence and independence which sustains one's existence. Hence, men are more likely to project beliefs relating to independence, while women are more likely to project beliefs relating to interdependence. In part, this difference may be explained by the different stratification position of males and females, as Gilligan (1982) suggests.

Overall, the responses suggest a duality in thinking. On the one hand, independence is a positive thing. On the other hand, there are necessary limits to this independence, and the respondents recognize these limits which necessitate a blending of work and welfare.

MOBILITY: THE UNEDUCATED AND UNTRAINED

For the second-to-the-lowest class, as for the lowest, education represents a crucial element in getting ahead. About 49 percent of the respondents mentioned inadequacies in education as an important cause of low status (see Table 4.3). The specific level of education generally identified as inadequate is that below high school graduation. This measure is slightly above the level of the lowest class, who are usually seen as having less than eighth-grade education.

The nature of the comments of the respondents do not emphasize lack of job and education as they do in reference to the lowest class, but rather the type of job and education. The second-lowest class is seen as having to accept jobs requiring only minimal skills because of their insufficient education (see Table 4.4).

The fact, however, that they are seen as still working corresponds to the view that they are still trying. It was because of these references that an additional code, "trying to get ahead," was added. It is important to note that trying to get ahead (Table 4.3B) is different from "trying," or making an effort in life (Table 4.2C). Ten percent of the respondents specifically mentioned the idea that the second-lowest class still has mobility aspirations and has hopes of rising in the class system, but there was no mobility rating for the lowest class (see Table 4.3B).

Overall, education continues to be seen as important for achieving a higher job level specifically, and to upward mobility in general. The second-lowest class would be expected to find more desirable jobs if it had more education. However, the responses present an internally contradictory element. If it is a

Table 4.3

Mobility: Proportion of Respondents by Class and Gender Who Mention Inadequate Education and Trying to Get Ahead as Characteristic of Second-Lowest Class Status (169 Respondents, Boston and Kansas City, 1971)

		Class Status				
	Upper	Upper Middle	Lower Middle	Upper Lower	Lower Lower	Total
A: Inadequate Education						
Women	100%	60%	81%	45%	57%	55%
Men	—	52%	39%	48%	—	44%
Total	33%	55%	49%	47%	44%	49%
B: "Trying to Get Ahead"						
Women	—	13%	7%	3%	—	6%
Men	—	10%	24%	7%	—	14%
Total	—	11%	16%	5%	—	10%

Table 4.4
Status: Proportions of Respondents by Class and Gender Who Mention Poor Job, Poor House/Neighborhood, and Impaired Lifestyle as Characteristic of the Second-Lowest Class (169 Respondents, Boston and Kansas City, 1971)

	Class Status					
	Upper	Upper Middle	Lower Middle	Upper Lower	Lower Lower	Total
A: Poor Nature of Job						
Women	—	53%	57%	58%	57%	56%
Men	100%	57%	55%	52%	—	54%
Total	66%	55%	56%	55%	44%	55%
B: Poor Character of House/Neighborhood						
Women	100%	66%	55%	64%	86%	63%
Men	100%	33%	61%	55%	—	52%
Total	100%	47%	57%	60%	66%	57%
C: Impaired Lifestyle						
Women	—	47%	39%	35%	—	35%
Men	—	9%	18%	14%	—	14%
Total	—	25%	28%	25%	—	24%

fact that more education is required to move ahead, then the lack of education would surely be a limiting factor on aspirations. Yet respondents also felt that one could hope for advancement even if, in reality, such hope would not be very well founded. This response conflict suggests the dualism inherent in the images around mobility in modern times. On the one hand, it is linked to education. On the other hand, it is linked to other elements, some more "luck related," which may have nothing to do with education. Indeed, the respondents themselves mentioned luck and "the breaks," many times, as has Jencks (1972) in his work, *Inequality*.

The emphasis on education generally declines as class levels decline, excepting the 33-percent response in the upper class (which represents only 1.5 persons so should not be given too much weight). While the drop is not dramatic, it is regular, from 55 percent mentioning something about education and not getting ahead in the upper-middle class to 44 percent of such mentions in the lower-lower class. It may be that the less the education of a respondent, the less he or she is apt to stress its importance, the women being more likely than men to mention lack of education as a detriment to achieving success. Their responses show a ragged irregular decrease by class level. Men, however, are more likely (14%) to mention mobility aspirations than women (6%). Once again, the position of the respondent in the class structure may be a relevant factor.

STATUS: THE IMPAIRED POOR

Class consciousness is one measure of status, and was discussed in Chapter 3. For this section, additional measures of status were developed to reflect the impaired life condition of the second-lowest class along three dimensions: job, house, and lifestyle in general.

The second-lowest class is perceived as having an inferior job; for example, jobs classified as domestic, custodial, janitorial, and the like. The jobs are not only low status, but one can see they have little objective security. It is for this reason that members of the second-lowest class were expected to occasionally need welfare. The jobs do not produce enough money to sustain the family, thus, supplemental charity is required. More than half of the respondents (55%) mentioned a low-status job as a characteristic of the second-lowest class (see Table 4.4A).

The low income produced by the job is doubtless a cause of the inferior housing and neighborhood which respondents mention as well (see Table 4.4B). Of the respondents, 57 percent noted that poor housing conditions, rented rather than owned, with inadequate facilities, overcrowding, and poor location, were other factors defining the second-lowest class. Some respondents, however, felt that this housing was the same as the working class (working class being one cut above the second-lowest class, or, in our terms, upper lower) but that the second-lowest class did not maintain the property.

Apart from housing and job, which were specific mentions, there were a series of general items which fell into a category called "impaired lifestyle" (see Table 4.4C). Though poor housing and a low-prestige job are both cause and result of the impaired lifestyle, the 24 percent who are represented here mentioned other deficiencies, such as lack of vacations, recreation, and travel, lack of opportunity for culture, lack of good food and proper clothing, and lack of other essentials, like a dependable car.

Women were more likely than men to mention home or neighborhood and lifestyle considerations, by margins of 63 percent to 52 percent and 35 percent to 14 percent, respectively. They described a bleak life, which embodies trying to make ends meet but not being able to do so.

The greater sensitivity of women to these matters is interesting. Women may more acutely feel the need for vacation, recreation, and so forth. These responses may reflect a desire for release from the treadmill of their role. On the other hand, it may reflect, for men, a lack of legitimacy or a sense of "okayness" to mention similar desires.

Table 4.5
Work: Proportions of Respondents by Class and Gender Who Mention Work as a Characteristic of the Second-Lowest Class (169 Respondents, Boston and Kansas City, 1971)

	Class Status					
	Upper	Upper Middle	Lower Middle	Upper Lower	Lower Lower	Total
Women	100%	87%	64%	55%	43%	63%
Men	100%	52%	60%	83%	50%	66%
Total	100%	66%	62%	68%	44%	65%

Overall, it appears that the next-lowest class is characterized by its effort, though it still falls short of the working class (whom we define as upper lower/lower middle), which has achieved some stability and luxuries, including home ownership and recreation options.

WORK: THE WORKING POOR

Without question, this sample of respondents perceives the second-lowest class as the working poor (see Table 4.5). The largest proportion, 65 percent, of the respondents mention working as the thing which distinguishes the second-lowest class from the lowest class. In some cases, it is all they mention. There is no important overall difference between men and women, but there is a slight class difference worth mentioning. Women are less apt to mention this factor as class decreases; for men, it is irregular.

A distinction should be made here between the working poor and the working class. As these respondents saw it, both held jobs, but the working poor had low status, temporary jobs, no union protection, and no real sense of security. However, the references did not seem to have the sense of permanence and fixity associated with a "class" position.

MORALISM: THE FAULT-FREE POOR

The negative moral flavor of the responses here is negligible, and largely consists of the exclusion from blame and fault (see Table 4.6). Only 3 percent of the respondents made any reference to fault or blame for the condition of being in the second-lowest class. The lack of censure, the absence of blame, is striking and clear. This finding perhaps links up with previous data which

Table 4.6
Moral: Proportions of Respondents by Class and Gender Who See Second-Lowest-Class Status as "Their Fault" or "Not Their Fault" (169 Respondents, Boston and Kansas City, 1971)

		Class Status				
	Upper	Upper Middle	Lower Middle	Upper Lower	Lower Lower	Total
A: "Their Fault"						
Women	—	6%	4%	6%	—	5%
Men	—	5%	—	—	—	1%
Total	—	5%	2%	3%	—	3%
B: "Not Their Fault"						
Women	—	6%	4%	3%	29%	7%
Men	—	—	9%	10%	—	7%
Total	33%	3%	7%	7%	22%	7%

stress trying and effort. But only 7 percent said it was "not their fault," with the exception of an unusual 22 percent of the lower-lower class. Overall, there are a few who specifically exclude them from blame, but most do not assign blame either.

As noted, where the responses suggest a slight direction, it is lack of fault. Only 7 percent of the respondents mentioned that those in the second-lowest class were not at fault on their position; 3 percent said that they were at fault.

These findings contrast sharply with those presented in Chapter 3 (see Table 3.6). There, almost 34 percent of the respondents mentioned that the lowest class was at fault. These differences are important.

STIGMA

Why should the lowest class be seen as morally negative while the second-lowest class avoids this stigma? For the second-lowest class, the absence of fault seems to suggest several points: The moral judgment appears to be linked to the belief that this class is making an effort; the respondents' belief that this group is working proves it. This difference in moral status is at the heart of the distinction between the worthy poor and the poor.

So powerful is the stigma against accepting charity or welfare that some people would rather steal than accept such funds. In a 1978 letter to Ann Landers published in the *Detroit Free Press*, a writer warns that "the little old ladies who steal to make ends meet and who would never accept charity will be prosecuted." It is a strange ethic when citizens view theft less negatively than charity. The idea that theft is better than welfare tells us much about American values.

INDIVIDUALISM AND ASCRIPTION

The extent to which respondents thought that individualism was involved in being in the second-lowest class was mild (see Table 4.7). Overall, only 7 percent of the respondents made any mention of individualism, which refers to those values relating to the "wholeness" of the individuals. Advancing age, illness, and family disorganization are conditions which threaten an individual's integrity to some degree. But respondents did not feel these elements were a factor here. Some mentioned that the second-lowest class included older persons, and a handful of persons mentioned that the second-lowest class had the father present, implying that in the lowest class the father was not present. But beyond these scanty references, individualism-type variables were rarely mentioned.

As for the ascriptive values, race was mentioned occasionally, but ethnicity and gender were simply not mentioned. Hence, the data in Table 4.8 reflect only the 7 percent of respondents who mentioned race as an element of the second-lowest class. However, the distribution of the responses is very interesting: 11 percent of the men, but only 1 percent of the women. These results correspond closely with the gender differences in race references to the lowest class (see Table 3.8). Another interesting aspect of the pattern (in spite of the small numbers), is that no one in the highest or lowest classes in the sample made any racial reference. This finding also occurred in the references to the lowest class. Hence, it seems to be upper-middle-class males, in

Table 4.7

Individualism: Proportions of Respondents by Class and Gender Who Mention Age, Illness, or Family Disorganization as Characteristic of the Second-Lowest Class (169 Respondents, Boston and Kansas City, 1971)

	Class Status					
	Upper	Upper Middle	Lower Middle	Upper Lower	Lower Lower	Total
Women	—	6%	14%	—	14%	7%
Men	—	5%	6%	7%	—	6%
Total	—	6%	10%	3%	11%	7%

Table 4.8
Ascription: Proportions of Respondents by Class and Gender Who Mention Race as a Characteristic of the Second-Lowest Class (169 Respondents, Boston and Kansas City, 1971)

| | Class Status | | | | |
	Upper	Upper Middle	Lower Middle	Upper Lower	Lower Lower	Total
Women	—	—	4%	—	—	1%
Men	—	33%	6%	3%	—	11%
Total	—	19%	5%	2%	—	7%

general, and lower-middle and upper-lower-class males, to a smaller extent, who associate race with class position in any descriptive or causal way. Why? Perhaps men, as the current primary competitors within the social structure, are more sensitive to issues of class and race than women.

Since the proportion of responses are low, however, these variables may be no more important in defining the second-lowest classes than in defining the lowest class. Despite the fact that ascriptive characteristics have been thought to be important, and may be in some instances, they are not in this sample.

DOMINANCE AND SUBDOMINANCE

Unlike the lowest class, the next-to-the-lowest class seems to be associated with dominant rather than subdominant values in the American system. The respondents tend to emphasize inner rather than other direction, and see the next-to-the-lowest class as in the mobility contest rather than as seeking the sponsorship of welfare bureaucracies. References suggest an achievement orientation is still present and operative here, as opposed to the lowest class, where no such references are made. The next-to-the-lowest class is seen as working, and there is an absence of negative moral tone and ambiance in the responses. The idea of "working poor" rather than "working class" suggests that the next-to-the-lowest class is a way station, and need not be permanent. What the responses suggest overall is that, however close the positions of lowest class and next-to-the-lowest class are on any sociological list, they are quite far apart in terms of social view, condition, and regard. Somehow, one has the sense that, to use academic parlance, being in the next to the lowest class is to get a social "C" grade. It is not great, but you get credit. Being in the lowest class is to get a social "D" grade; one does not receive any credit. This difference is a big one in school and in life.

THE OVERALL STRUCTURE OF RANKINGS

What happens to the total overall rankings if classes are combined? This combination allows us to look at values rankings (see Table 4.10). It appears that the remarks fall into about three main groups. The highest groups, work, mobility, status, and independence, are mentioned by at least 30 percent of the respondents. In a middle group is one value arena, moral, mentioned by an average of 13.5 percent of respondents.

Last are the value arenas of integrity and ascription, with very low proportions of mentions. This overall ranking is similar to the rankings of each of the lowest classes, but far from identical. The perceptions toward those at the bottom, whether in the lowest or second-lowest position, have some very important differences.

People appear to think about both lower classes in the same terms, and with similar frameworks. The way these terms are applied, however, and the attribution of certain characteristics to one class but not to the other are important. In thinking about the two classes, values themselves do not disappear but merely shift in application. It is this configuration which becomes the pattern of culture, either of a particular group or with respect to a particular group. The configurational shift within the same value framework is the key element.

CONCLUSION

What these results suggest is that welfare has two meanings to Americans: dominant and subdominant, negative and less negative. The dominant nega-

Table 4.10
Overall Average Rankings of Value Characteristics of the Two Lowest Classes (200 Respondents, Boston and Kansas City, 1971)

Lowest and Second-Lowest Value Characteristics	Percentage Mentioned
Work	47.0
Mobility	37.0
Status	32.0
Independence	31.0
Moral	13.5
Integrity	7.5
Ascription	5.0

Note: Moral Values score is 27 percent if the mentions of "fault" are added together, rather than averaged.

tive orientation assumes that welfare is synonymous with giving up and means no longer trying or caring. It is associated, in this case, with not working. The other view of welfare is more accepting, and assumes that it is a necessary but occasional supplement to working wages. The work versus welfare clash thus can be interpreted from these data as one of effort versus lack of effort.

In sum, the image of the near-poor tends to emphasize the dominant aspects of the American value system, and this emphasis creates a large social gap between the lowest class and the next-to-the-lowest class. This social space is the difference between being accepted and unaccepted. While at first the empirical differences may seem small—the difference between having or not having a job—the perceptions of the general public seem to reflect a more serious, deeper chasm.

Chapter 5

The Overseer of the Poor: View from the County Welfare Office

In Chapters 3 and 4, the views of the public at large toward the poor and the near-poor revealed a structure of attitudes which sharply differentiated those "on welfare" from those "getting a little help from the government." This distinction appears to be based upon moral entitlement to benefits, related in turn to the extent of contribution the recipient appears to be making, and whether the recipient is "trying."

It is important, then, to explore the views of one with great responsibility for providing these contested social benefits: the county welfare director. What are the director's views of recipients, and what does he or she think are the views of the general public? Do the same themes persist here as emerged in Chapters 3 and 4?

WHERE DO THE DATA COME FROM?

These data come from responses to a questionnaire entitled "To Provide Hope," which was sent to a random sample of county welfare directors (N = 340) and, where appropriate, child welfare agency directors (N = 70), around the country in 1969 (Sarri 1970; Silberman 1970; Benjamin 1977). Of the total questionnaires distributed, 240 were returned and, of those, 225 were sufficiently complete to be usable in this analysis. Two sets of questions are relevant here in revealing the attitudes and judgments of the public welfare directors.

The first set was a group of statements about welfare recipients and services with which respondents could indicate their level of agreement. One example is the following:

#39. Welfare Recipients, by and large, lead an easy life.

The code ranged from strongly agree (1) to strongly disagree (6). On the example item, respondents scored an average of 5.5, which is well toward the strongly disagree end.

The second set asked respondents to indicate the extent to which each of a variety of adjectives applied to AFDC. A list of words containing adjectives such as the following was provided:

13.	Decent	96%
5.	Deserving	95%
12.	Immoral	33%
9.	Lazy	36%

Respondents were asked to rate the proportion of recipients for whom they thought the word applied. Proportions—the ones in the list are actual findings—tell the tale. The welfare directors thought the term "decent" applied to 96 percent of AFDC recipients, while the term "lazy" applied to 36 percent.

The directors were asked for two separate ratings on the first set of items. One was for themselves; a second was to rate what they thought their friends thought. On the second set of items, directors were also asked for two sets of ratings. Again, their own views were requested, but they were also asked to report what they thought "people in general" were thinking. The following list outlines the areas where information is available:

	Directors	Friends	People in General
Set 1 (general statements)	X	X	No
Set 2 (adjectives)	X	No	X

We also attempt to use some aspects of the respondent's personal status and background. This helps to predict the structure of attitudes held and perceived on the basis of personal characteristics.

Finally, data were used from the city/county data book for relevant counties, so one could assess the extent to which wealth, education of the counties, and the like might affect the attitudes of the directors. Where there was variation in the perceived attitudes of friends and people in general, it was of interest to see if that variance could be accounted for by factual differences in the community composition or by other, personal differences.

A Few Cautions

As in every data collection of a national sort, there are some caveats. Although every county did not return the questionnaire, the counties that did not return the questionnaire are not demographically different from those that did.

Nearly all respondents were the county welfare directors themselves. In a few of the larger county agencies, it appears that the director asked a subordinate to fill out at least part of the instrument.

In addition, the response categories were not identical in Set 2. For the directors themselves, five categories of response were available: They could say, "I believe this applies to Most; Some; Few; Hardly Any." However, the directors could only respond "yes" or "no" when asked if various adjectives applied to people in general. One does not know the extent to which these two types of response categories might have biased the response framework. Even the categories on the directors' side did not lend themselves to an unambiguous interpretation. It was assumed that "few" and "hardly any" were equivalent to "no," but that judgment could be questioned.

Methodology

In simple terms, the answers were examined by a technique called factor analysis, which uses a computer to see if there are any underlying dimensions within a range of answers. For example, on an intelligence test, several correct answers may group together into a factor or dimension called "math ability," and others may group together into a factor or dimension called "verbal ability." One can then look at the dimension instead of specific questions. Once dimensions are developed, explorations can then be made concerning what factors explain high ratings on them. One group, for example, might score well on math factors, while another group might score well on verbal dimension. Four factor analyses, one for each package of directors' responses, were completed. In the tables for this chapter, we retained only those variables which correlated in a statistically significant way with the factors developed.

THE DIRECTOR'S PERCEPTIONS OF THE POOR

The general perception the directors had of the welfare poor was quite positive. They seem to think of them as decent folks, if a bit immature, for whom the jobs are not there.

It Is Not Their Fault

The dimension that emerged as embodying the directors views of the poor is one I called "external cause of poverty." What it really means is that the welfare directors had positive views of the poor, and felt they had a hard life and were folks who could not find work. Pushing things a bit in terms of the material in Chapter 4, I conclude that the directors are telling us, "It is not their fault" (see Table 5.1, D1).

With respect to the directors' views toward AFDC mothers, two dimensions emerged (see Table 5.2, D3, D4), both positive in nature. The first dimension (D3) shows the directors rate the recipients as deserving and decent, while disagreeing with words like immoral, exploiting taxpayers, stupid, and lazy. I call that "positive moral status."

Table 5.1
Factor Structure of County Public Welfare Directors' Own General Attitudes (National Sample, 1969)

Q. No.	Items[a]	Loading[b]	Mean
Factor D1: External Cause of Parenting			
44. If a person tried hard enough he could find work and support himself.		.72	4.6
21. Except when there is a depression, anyone in our country can get a job if he really tries.		.64	4.8
39. Welfare recipients, by and large, live an easy life.		.56	5.5
34. Welfare recipients generally are unwilling to accept responsibilities		.54	4.8
24. Having to struggle for what you get in life is the best way to develop character.		.54	4.0
47. When a married couple with children is having serious problems getting along together, their first consideration should be to keep the family together at all costs.		.49	4.0
48. Welfare recipients are basically inadequate people.		.40	4.3
Factor D2: Positive Status of Agency			
30. Most clients think we are doing a pretty good job.		-.64	2.9
28. It's a public stigma to accept help from our agency.		.53	4.1
27. Most people respect welfare workers.		-.50	3.0
42. Welfare workers, by and large, fail to respect the client's private life.		.49	4.4
Eigenvalue = 1.74 (N = 215)			

[a]Responses to original items were on a six-point scale from 1= Strongly Agree to 6= Strongly Disagree. Thus, high scores indicate disagreement with the item as worded.

[b]Loadings obtained after Varimax rotation.

Table 5.2
Factor Structure of County Public Welfare Directors' Attitudes toward AFDC Mothers (National Sample, 1969)

Q. No.	Item[a]	Loading[b]	Percentage Who Say It Applies to Most or Some
Factor D3: Positive Moral Status			
11.	Exploiting Taxpayers	−0.74	18
12.	Immoral	−0.74	33
9.	Lazy	−0.73	36
15.	Dishonest	−0.73	23
17.	Greedy	−0.73	19
4.	Scheming	−0.70	28
14.	Stupid	−0.65	21
3.	Promiscuous	−0.62	44
5.	Decent	−0.43	96
13.	Deserving	0.42	95
7.	Immature	−0.41	82
	Eigenvalue = 5.40 (N = 223)		
Factor D4: Positive Effort			
19.	Hardworking	0.80	92
16.	Conscientious	0.60	93
10.	Maternal	0.54	93
6.	Responsible	0.52	94
20.	Grateful	0.49	86
8.	Religious	0.43	75
18.	Family-minded	0.40	94
	Eigenvalue = 2.30 (N = 223)		

[a]Responses to original items on a four-point scale indicate that the item applies to Most (1), Some (2), Few (3), or Hardly Any (4).

[b]Loadings obtained after Varimax rotation.

In the second dimension, which I call "positive effort," directors see recipients as hardworking, conscientious, maternal, and responsible. They also see them as grateful, religious, and family minded. Both of these dimensions suggest that, as persons, directors have a positive view of their clientele.

The Agency Is Doing a Good Job

A second dimension emerged which related to the directors' views of their own agencies (see Table 5.1, D2). The directors think their clients think they are doing a good job, and disagree with the view that it is a stigma to receive help from the agency. This particular view is in sharp contrast with the views expressed by the residents of Boston and Kansas City in Chapters 3 and 4, which suggest stigma, or, at best, grudging acceptance.

What My Friends Think

Data with respect to directors' perceptions of what their friends think are somewhat different from their own (see Table 5.3, F1). This dimension I called "internal cause of poverty." Directors perceive their friends as taking more of the potentially negative individual responsibility view, such as "Any able-bodied individual who refuses to take a job should not receive assistance." They see their friends as taking essentially the opposite of the external control view. My guess is they are probably right in that assessment, but it can make for stress, as the directors have a different value set than they perceive their friends to have.

On the other hand, directors believe their friends think the agency is well regarded by clients and that their staff is underpaid. It might be a sort of "you are doing the best job you can under difficult circumstances" view.

People in General Think Negative Thoughts

On the other hand, however, directors' views of the ideas people in general have are rather negative (see Table 5.4). They suggest negative effort or, as I referred to it, "lack of effort" (P1) and, indeed, suggest very negative perceptions; I call it "negative moral status" (P2). In this assessment, the directors reflect the kind of views expressed by the Boston and Kansas City residents. An intercorrelation matrix of relationships between the factors is in Table 5.5.

In sum, the directors' views are positive and sympathetic toward welfare mothers, and positive as well toward their agency and its programs. The directors' views also stress external causes of poverty, a view the directors recognize as unpopular with the public at large.

ATTITUDINAL CORRELATES: CHARACTERISTICS, COMPETENCIES, CONDITIONS, AND CONTEXTS

In an earlier analysis of behavior (Tropman 1989), the simultaneous impact of personal characteristics, personal competencies, organizational conditions, and organizational contexts was seen as important. This scheme has some applicability to the explanation of welfare directors' attitudes.

Table 5.3
Factor Structure of County Public Welfare Directors' Perceptions of Their Friends' Central Attitudes (National Sample, 1969)

Q. No.	Item[a]	Loading[b]	Mean
Factor F1: Internal Cause of Poverty			
44.	If a person tried hard enough he could find work and support himself.	0.77	2.6
39.	Welfare recipients, by and large, live an easy life.	0.69	3.4
21.	Except when there is a depression anyone in our country can get a job if he really tried.	0.68	2.6
41.	Very few clients will ask for help unless they really need it.	−0.62	4.1
34.	Welfare recipients generally are unwilling to accept responsibilities.	0.62	2.8
36.	Any able-bodied individual who refuses to take a job should not receive assistance.	0.60	1.9
24.	Having to struggle for what you get in life is the best way to develop character.	0.58	2.4
48.	Welfare recipients are basically inadequate people.	0.55	3.0
40.	I don't think our agency can learn much from the clients it serves.	0.53	3.7
32.	By and large, black welfare workers should take care of black clients.	0.45	3.8
31.	Welfare recipients should not be entitled to vote.	0.44	5.0
47.	When a married couple with children is having serious problems getting along together, their first consideration should be to keep the family together at all costs.	0.43	3.2
46.	Some welfare workers are too lenient with their clients.	0.41	2.3
26.	I don't like the idea of letting clients tell us how to run this palace.	0.41	2.4
	Eigenvalue = 5.75 (N = 166)		
Factor F2: Positive Status of Agency			
30.	Most clients think we are doing a pretty good job.	0.47	4.3
35.	Welfare workers are not adequately paid for the work they do.	0.44	4.8
	Eigenvalue = 1.24 (N = 186)		

[a]Responses to original items were on a six-point scale from 1 = Strongly Agree to 6 = Strongly Disagree. Thus, high scores indicate disagreement with the item as worded.

[b]Loadings obtained after Varimax rotation.

Table 5.4
Factor Structure of County Public Welfare Directors' Perceptions of People in General's Attitudes Toward AFDC Mothers (National Sample, 1969)

Q. No.	Item[a]	Loading[b]	Percentage Who Perceive That People in General Believe It Applies
Factor P1: Lack of Effort			
16.	Conscientious	0.77	13
5.	Decent	0.70	23
6.	Responsible	0.61	11
8.	Religious	0.55	8
13.	Deserving	0.49	15
20.	Grateful	0.48	13
10.	Maternal	0.44	42
1.	Unfortunate	0.41	56
18.	Family-minded	0.41	30
	Eigenvalue = 6.01 (N = 225)		
Factor P2: Negative Moral Status			
11.	Exploiting Taxpayers	−0.76	87
15.	Dishonest	−0.67	76
12.	Immoral	−0.61	91
3.	Promiscuous	−0.58	91
4.	Scheming	−0.56	76
9.	Lazy	−0.56	93
17.	Greedy	−0.55	74
13.	Deserving	0.44	15
	Eigenvalue = 1.19 (N = 225)		

[a]Responses to original items were Yes = 1; No = 5.
[b]Loadings obtained after Varimax rotation.

Data which report on the relationships among personal characteristics and competencies of the welfare director, organizational characteristics of the department, and characteristics of the county are presented in Table 5.6. The numbers are standardized beta coefficients between a particular variable and a particular factor.

What are the overall results? Which of the areas—characteristics, competencies, conditions, or contexts—predict directors' attitudes most strongly?

Table 5.5
Correlations among Attitude Factors (AFDC Mothers, National Sample, 1969)

Factors	D1	D2	D3	D4	F1	F2	P1	P2
Directors								
D1 (External Cause of Poverty)	1.00							
D2 (Positive Status of Agency)	.00	1.00						
D3 (Positive Moral Status)	−.24**	−.01	1.00					
D4 (Positive Effort)	-.25**	.00	-.05	1.00				
Friends								
F1 (Internal Cause of Poverty)	.18*	.00	.17*	.00	1.00			
F2 (Positive Status of Agency)	.35**	−.25**	.00	−.04	−.06	1.00		
People in General								
P1 (Lack of Effort)	.09	−.29**	.18*	.11	−.04	.20**	1.00	
P2 (Negative Moral Status)	−.09	−.10	.06	−.09	−.18	−.02	.14	1.00

N = 165; *p .05; **p .01.

It is context by a nose (average beta of 0.13; a range from 0.01 to 0.57). Conditions, competence, and characteristics each had means of 0.09, 0.06, and 0.08, respectively. What this suggests is that the directors' perceptions do not change a lot depending on themselves, the nature of the training they have had, the kind of agency where they work, or even their county.

A different approach (see Table 5.7) would be to look at proportion of significant (statistically) relationships in the total matrix in question. The personal characteristics and competencies do not explain much about the directors' views (less than 5% of the betas were significant). Organizational and contextual variables explain a bit of the directors' own views as well the perceptions they have of friends and, then, people in general (significance of 12.5% and 15.3%, respectively). Strength increases as one moves to the lower-right-hand corner of the matrix (context/people in general). Contextual variables are more influential in accounting for the directors' views of people in general. Outside variables, it seems, influence the perception of the views of outside people, but the overall strength is not great in any event.

Yet they did have perceptions. We could, of course, have used the wrong independent variables. More likely, though, they are partaking of a national culture of attitudes toward the poor.

Another approach would be to ask if, though the independent variables do not stand out, can we predict much about the factors when thye are taken together. Here, again, the answer is no. The results (called R^2) are in the form

Table 5.6
Standardized Beta Coefficients Predicting Factor Index (County Public Welfare Directors, National Sample, 1969)

Personal, Organizational, and Community Variables	Directors' Own Attitudes				Directors' Friends		People in General	
	External Cause of Poverty D1 (N = 181)	Positive View of Agency D2 (N = 181)	Positive Moral Status D3 (N = 179)	Positive Effort D4 (N = 179)	Internal Cause of PM F1 (N = 155)	Positive View of Agency F2 (N = 155)	Negative Effort P1 (N = 181)	Negative Moral Status P2 (N = 181)
Personal Characteristics								
Age	0.05	0.16	0.04	-0.18	0.03	0.13	-0.09	-0.11
Tenure	-0.16	-0.05	-0.05	-0.17	-0.18	-0.06	0.06	-0.03
Income	0.07	0.02	-0.05	0.18	-0.16	0.06	0.29*	0.03
White	0.11	0.03	-0.10	0.05	-0.09	0.01	-0.02	0.05
Male	-0.09	0.01	0.06	-0.16	0.01	-0.03	0.10	-0.04
Pol Pref	0.17	-0.01	-0.01	0.07	0.08	0.08	-0.18*	0.08
x = 0.08								
Personal Competence								
MSW	0.02	-0.11	-0.07	-0.07	-0.01	-0.02	-0.14	0.03
x = 0.06								
Organizational Conditions								
Total Staff	0.10	-0.18	-0.03	-0.14	0.08	0.03	-0.08	-0.02
Complaint Index	-0.04	-0.27***	-0.02	-0.15	-0.11	0.03	0.15*	0.04
x = 0.08								

Demographic Context

Urban–Rural	-0.05	-0.08	-0.01	0.02	0.19	-0.03	-0.01	-0.07
Median Income	0.03	-0.18	0.14	-0.27	0.14	-0.11	0.21	-0.01
Percentage Nonwhite	0.02	0.20*	0.36***	0.05	0.20	-0.09	-0.11	-0.11
Percentage Foreign-Born	-0.01	0.21*	0.09	0.11	0.11	0.30**	-0.12	-0.11
Median Age	0.10	-0.02	-0.06	-0.15	0.16	-0.20*	-0.08	0.02
Population Density	-0.19*	-0.01	0.01	0.07	0.01	-0.29**	-0.02	0.08
Percentage Industrialized	0.08	-0.07	-0.12	-0.06	-0.06	-0.03	0.17	0.02
Percentage Voting Democrat	0.13	-0.16*	-0.06	-0.01	0.02	0.20*	0.09	0.01
Percentage 5 Years Education	-0.04	0.06	0.03	-0.16	-0.18	0.16	0.25*	0.20
Percentage Crowding	0.03	0.19	-0.16	-0.12	-0.01	-0.32*	-0.32*	-0.11
Percentage with TV	0.16	0.57***	0.05	0.05	0.03	-0.14	-0.36**	-0.02
Farm Level of Living	-0.17	-0.04	-0.06	0.10	0.03	0.01	-0.36***	0.13
x = 0.13								
Mult. R.	0.40	0.58	0.38	0.36	0.38	0.57	0.48	0.26
R²	0.16	0.34	0.14	0.13	0.15	0.26	0.23	0.07
Significance	0.10	0.001	0.21	0.33	0.36	0.01	0.01	0.94
	+	+	+	+	sl.+	sl.–	–	–

Note: * = p 0.05; ** = p 0.01, *** = p 0.001; + = positive; sl = slightly; – = negative.

Table 5.7
Proportions of Significant Variables, Regression Matrix of Personal, Organizational, and Demographic Variables Predicting to Directors' Own Attitudes, Directors' Perceptions of Friend's Attitudes, and Directors' Perception of Attitudes of People in General (National Sample, 1969)

Independent Variables Clusters	Director's Own Attitudes	Perception of Friends	People in General	Total
Charactistics (N = 6)	0.0%	0.0%	9.5%	4.2%
Competencies (N = 1)	0.0%	0.0%	0.0%	0.0%
Organizational Conditions (N = 2)	12.5%	0.0%	25.0%	12.5%
Demographic Context (N = 12)	10.4%	20.8%	16.6%	15.6%
Total	9.5%	11.9%	16.6%	11.3%

Note: Many colleagues would not consider 34%, for example, to be all that "bad." While it is within the usual range for much social science, an R^2 of 50% seems to be reasonable to strive for.

of a percentage (Table 5.6 at the bottom) which tells us the fraction of the dependent variable a series of independent variables can explain (10% would be low; 90% high). Results here are not encouraging. Ranging from a low of 7 percent to a high of 34 percent of the variance explained, one must conclude that we cannot explain much about the directors' attitudes. This result supports the notion that the directors are drawing from general, society-wide points of view which they have adopted as their own (at least for purposes of the questionnaire), and that these views are not substantially modified by their own characteristics, the agency, or the community in which they live.[1]

CONCLUSION

The welfare directors' views of the poor and their own role in the poverty establishment is in several ways much like that of the Boston and Kansas City respondents: Effort, fault, and morality are all important components (though directors had a more positive views of welfare recipients than the respondents from Boston and Kansas City). The same cognitive elements recur in thinking about the less advantaged. Further, since some of the items referred to one's stance toward the world in general, the link between attitudes toward the poor and more general postures is strengthened. The directors seemed accurate in perceiving a negative public image of the welfare client, but they also felt positive about their agency and that there was no public stigma in accepting help from it. As Chapter 6 will indicate, this view is somewhat in error, at least with respect to a survey of Detroit women. They rated a public welfare agency poorly in comparison to a private agency. Directors are probably somewhat biased where their own agencies are concerned.

The directors report positive attitudes toward their agencies and toward their welfare clients, whom they view as morally upright and hard triers. They represent, as noted, the reverse of the attitudes they ascribed to people in general. What is possible, however, is that the positive mythology also serves a function or purpose for the director. Everyone needs to feel that they are making a contribution to society. Welfare directors, as advocates for the disadvantaged, need to feel positively toward their clients and toward the role their agency plays in assisting them. These views protect them against accusations that welfare is harmful. They also believe external control is necessary, a viewpoint which protects their job and makes it meaningful. The logical inconsistencies inherent in these two views should not be overlooked (D1, D3, and D4; there is no control dimension of people in general). Perhaps they are saying that the clients are of good moral status and do try to improve their lot, but, since external control elements are so crucial, their efforts have limited value. Self-help is thus beyond their control and, by implication, help is beyond the control of the welfare directors as well. It is as if they can see themselves as able to assist a flood victim but powerless to stop the flood.

These data were collected in 1969. From the perspective of more than twenty-five years, we can see, during the very time of the Great Society, the perception of public negativity. County directors were putting a good face on it and keeping their chin up, but even they recognized they were bucking the tide. Even their friends did not think as they did. It is no surprise, then, or should be no surprise, that "ending welfare as we know it" in 1996 can be seen as a case of structural lag catching up. The culture is more negative than the structure. The structure changed; not right away, but in time.

NOTE

1. These results concerning the impact of social structure on policy attitudes is essentially the same type of finding as reported in the book, *Public Policy Opinion and the Elderly* (Tropman 1987).

Chapter 6

Mothers: Opinions and Stereotypes

The views of welfare directors about clients and their views of what the opinions people in general hold about welfare stimulates one to wonder what people at about the same time thought welfare recipients were like. Fortunately, some data are available, using a 1964 survey of Detroit mothers. These data are of interest for several interrelated reasons. First, of course, they allow us to compare people in general with the views of welfare directors on people in general, even though the mothers were interviewed in 1964 and the welfare directors in 1969. Second, it provides a look at pre-riot Detroit.

To look at what urban residents, that is, women with children who would be eligible for AFDC, thought about the program, is of some interest. Further, differences in view by race, social class of neighborhood, and whether or not they had been users of the program would be of interest and contribute to an understanding of who thinks what and why.

Important, too, though, is a comparison of these views with those toward private agencies. Private volunteer social agencies were the first line of defense against poverty before the government programs developed in the 1930s. Today they still play a vital role in providing social services to their communities. These services tend to be more focused on personal counseling and interpersonal helping and there is much argument that they will again become the first line of defense.

By definition, public welfare agencies work only with those in financial need, whereas the concept of need which might bring one into contact with a private agency is much broader, and can include psychosocial problems other than financial. Stereotypes of voluntary agencies see them as more innovative, personal, and less bureaucratic than private ones. But there have been allegations over the years that private social welfare agencies are "leaving" the poor and focusing on middle-class clients (Cloward and Epstein 1967). While there is certainly some likelihood of this emphasis in some agencies, others continue to serve the lowest class and the next-to-the-lowest class as well as the middle and upper-middle class (see Chapters 3 and 4). The data from Detroit allow inspection of public and private agencies and the views of mothers toward them.

SOURCE OF DATA

The data used in this report comes from a sample of families drawn from the Detroit, Michigan, area for the Great Cities School Improvement Project in 1964. From a total of 18 school districts, a random sample of fifth and sixth grade children were selected. Their mothers—1,536 in all—were interviewed.

Specifically, I am looking at responses to the following questions:

We've been talking about several different types of organizations. Now I am going to read to you a list of organizations and groups that people have different ideas about. After each one, I want you to think about the people who work for these organizations, and tell if they are doing an excellent job, a good, a fair job, or a poor job in serving the public. The ADC or Detroit Department of Welfare? Private Social Agencies, like Family Service and Child Guidance Clinics?

The possible answers to these questions were "excellent," "good," "fair," "poor," and "don't know." For purposes of analysis, the "excellent" and "good" categories have been combined into a positive rating, and the "fair" and "poor" responses have been combined into a negative rating. I report the responses in several ways. Sometimes I present the proportions expressing positive or negative opinions, while other times categories of "opinion expressed" or "don't know" responses suffice. When I refer to the proportion of respondents which is aware of an agency type, the positive and negative responses will be summarized; the "don't know" responses have been excluded.

WHAT DID PEOPLE THINK?

In Detroit in 1964, 72 percent of the sample had an opinion about public agencies, while only 48 percent had an opinion about private agencies (see Table 6.1). Of those who did have an opinion, a much larger proportion expressed a positive view of the work of the private agency than about the ADC/welfare agency (81% versus 56% said excellent or good; see Table 6.2).

From a current perspective, however, the picture may be quite different. On the negative side, with so many questions being raised about the salaries

Table 6.1

Opinions about Social Agencies Services (Detroit Women, 1964)

Agency	Total	Excellent	Good	Fair	Poor	Don't Know	N
ADC/Welfare	100%	7%	33%	20%	12%	28%	1536
Private	100%	9%	30%	8%	1%	52%	1536

Note: Since all respondents answered each question, the grand total is 1536.

of private-agency executives and agency integrity, the view could be significantly less positive. On the other hand, public agencies are coming under attack, from schools to the welfare department. In Michigan, the Department of Social Services was changed to the Family Independence Agency, and may disappear as part of ending welfare as we know it. Private agencies, as well as businesses, are taking over through outsourcing and privitization of many previously public functions. The picture of which organization does what kind of work has become quite murky.

OPINIONS AND USE OF AGENCY SERVICE

Women who had used the agency service are more likely to have an opinion about it (see Tables 6.3 and 6.4). While the famous sociologist George Caspar Homans (1950, 43) suggested, "interaction breeds affection," that was not always true here. Those who used private agencies felt very positive (84%). Those women who had used public agencies felt less positive (58%). Strike one for Homans. And it seems that about the same proportions (80% and 53%) felt the same way, even if they had not been clients. Strike two for Homans. In fact, use did not make much difference. This finding is much like the one for the welfare directors. There are views, but personal experience does not seem to drive them in the way Homans suggested. Perhaps we need to look more at the quality of the experiences and the nature of the interaction, rather than interaction by itself.[1]

Table 6.2

Opinions of Knowledgeable Respondents about Social Agencies' Services (Detroit Women, 1964)

Agency	Total	Excellent	Good	Fair	Poor	N
ADC/Welfare	100%	10%	46%	28%	16%	1106
Private	100%	19%	62%	16%	2%	736

Table 6.3
Opinions about Social Agency Service by Use of Service (Detroit Women, 1964)

Race	Total	Positive	Negative	Don't Know	N
ADC/Welfare					
Used	100%	57%	40%	3%	390
Not Used	100%	34%	29%	37%	1146
Private					
Used	100%	67%	13%	20%	85
Not Used	100%	37%	9%	54%	1451

Table 6.4
Opinions of Knowledgeable Respondents about Social Agencies' Service by Use of Servce (Detroit Women, 1964)

Agency	Total	Positive	Negative	N
ADC/Welfare				
Used	100%	58%	42%	385
Not Used	100%	53%	47%	721
Private				
Used	100%	84%	16%	68
Not Used	100%	80%	20%	668

OPINIONS AND EDUCATION OF MOTHER

Education of the respondent does not make much of a difference either. About 50 percent of the respondents think that ADC/welfare agencies are doing a good job, while 87 percent think that the private social agencies are doing good work (see Tables 6.5 and 6.6).

OPINIONS AND RACE OF RESPONDENT

For this survey, in 1964, race matters. Forty percent of the white respondents had no opinion about ADC/welfare agencies, compared with only 15 percent of the non-white (African American) group. Of those who had an opinion (Tables 6.7 and 6.8), 56 percent of the whites and 54 percent of the non-whites were favorable.

Table 6.5
**Opinions of Knowledgeable Respondents about ADC/Welfare Agencies'
Service by Education of Mother (Detroit Women, 1964)**

Education	Total	Positive	Negative	N
Some College	100%	50%	50%	76
High School	100%	54%	46%	748
Eighth Grade or Less	100%	49%	51%	282

Table 6.6
**Opinions of Knowledgeable Respondents about Private Social
Agencies' Service by Education of Mother (Detroit Women, 1964)**

Education	Total	Positive	Negative	N
Some College	100%	87%	13%	72
High School	100%	97%	3%	490
Eighth Grade or Less	100%	76%	24%	176

Table 6.7
**Opinions about ADC/Welfare Agencies' Service by Race (Detroit Women,
1964)**

Race	Total	Positive	Negative	Don't Know	N
White	100%	34%	26%	40%	867
Non-White	100%	48%	33%	15%	679

For private agencies, a somewhat similar picture emerges. In the total group, whites were slightly more apt to give a favorable rating (85% versus 76%; see Tables 6.9 and 6.10).

OPINIONS AND NEIGHBORHOOD SOCIAL CLASS

The sample consisted of twelve lower-class and six middle-class school districts, selected on the basis of income and education levels within the neighborhood. Here again, the independent variable did not matter much; women in both lower-class and middle-class neighborhoods were much more positive about private agencies than public ones (81% versus 54.5%; see Tables 6.11 and 6.12).

Table 6.8
Opinions of Knowledgeable Respondents about ADC/Welfare Agencies'
Service by Race (Detroit Women, 1964)

Race	Total	Positive	Negative	N
White	100%	56%	44%	520
Non-white	100%	54%	46%	577

Table 6.9
Opinions About Private Agencies' Service by Race (Detroit Women, 1964)

Race	Total	Positive	Negative	Don't Know	N
White	100%	42%	5%	53%	867
Non-white	100%	35%	12%	53%	679

PUBLIC KNOWLEDGE/PUBLIC SUPPORT

The most interesting result is that private agencies are well regarded in 1964, regardless of the characteristics of the respondent. It suggests that the opinions of agency functions and the staff performance may well be based on factors other than experience. Such variables as race, education, neighborhood class, and agency use do not make much difference either. Welfare as we knew it had minimal support among Detroit women in the mid-1960s, even among those who used the program.

Women in Detroit, therefore, have a similar opinion structure to that of welfare directors from around the country and the perception those directors have of welfare matters. For the Detroit women, as for the mostly male agency directors, there was little influence of experiential, personal, or demographic factors. The image of social services, public or private, seems to come from sources within the general culture.

In one area, however, these data allow us to access the views reported by the welfare directors. The directors believed that clients felt their agency was doing a "good job" (see Table 5.1, item 30). Data here (Table 6.4) calls the directors' view into question to some extent. Their own clients, in 1964 in Detroit, thought only moderately well of the agency, and their views were only slightly more favorable than those who had no experience with the agency (see Table 6.2). If 50 percent of one's clients think one is doing a good or excellent job, perhaps that is sufficient. On the other hand, there are no overall evaluative norms with which to make a comparison. However, 81 percent

Table 6.10
Opinions of Knowledgeable Respondents about Private Social Agencies'
Service by Race (Detroit Women, 1964)

Race	Total	Positive	Negative	N
White	100%	85%	15%	420
Non-white	100%	76%	24%	316

Table 6.11
Opinions about Social Agencies' Service by Social Class of Neighborhood
(Detroit Women, 1964)

Agency and Class	Total	Positive	Negative	Don't Know	N
ADC					
Middle	100%	29%	27%	44%	511
Lower	100%	44%	35%	21%	1025
Private					
Middle	100%	44%	13%	43%	511
Lower	100%	36%	8%	66%	1025

of the respondents rated private agencies as good or excellent. Hence, the welfare directors are not perceiving their clients accurately.

CONCLUSION

In the middle of the 1960 period, Detroit women with children in school did not have a very favorable view toward public agencies and were somewhat more favorable to private agencies, though many fewer knew about the latter group. Various characteristics of the respondents did not seem to make a difference, including the important ones of education, race, and class. Stereotypes seem to be dominating the views of women about the social service system.

Relating these findings to that which has gone before, a troubling picture emerges. It is possible to think that, among Detroit women, welfare is for the lowest class and private agencies are for the next-to-the-lowest class, as discussed in Chapters 3 and 4. If true, this perception suggests a great gulf, and one that would be easy to exploit in an anti-welfare, hate-the-poor mindset.

This view—limited support—of public agencies, is echoed by the directors of public agencies themselves. While the directors have positive per-

Table 6.12
Opinions of Knowledgeable Respondents about Social Agencies' Service by Social Class of Neighborhood (Detroit, 1964)

Agency and Class	Total	Positive	Negative	N
ADC[a]				
Middle	100%	52%	48%	287
Lower	100%	57%	43%	807
Private				
Middle	100%	79%	21%	288
Lower	100%	83%	17%	448

[a]Twelve knowledgeable respondents could not be analyzed on this question, giving an N of 1094 instead of 1106.

sonal attitudes (Chapter 5), they believe their friends and people in general do not like their agency or their clients. To make matters somewhat worse, they appear to have misperceived the support their own clients have for them. This picture is certainly a problematic one.

As we look at it from the perspectives of the late 1990s, it becomes more obvious why President Clinton signed the welfare bill. His reading was that there was limited support—politically—for welfare. These data suggest that was true even during the heyday of the Great Society, the time when, other things being equal, one would expect the greatest support for welfare. Yet even then, the country as a whole (as seen in Boston and Kansas City) distinguished sharply between those who were "on welfare" (the status poor) and those who needed "a little help from the government."

Putting these pieces together suggests that American society has a broad, situation-independent view of the poor, and it is negative. When I say that America hates the poor, it appears that even the poor may hate the poor.

NOTE

1. Homans's observation is one formulation of the theory of "cognitive dissonance," a theory that suggests that, over time, values come into conformity with and support actions. Readers know this is true, sometimes. But it is not the only thing that is true. Sometimes actions change because of values, and sometimes actions (accepting welfare from the welfare department, for example) and values (liking it) never meet.

Part III

THE LIFE CYCLE POOR: IMAGES OF THE AGED

The image of the old—the life cycle poor—shares much with that of the status poor. Being old and being at the bottom of the status ladder are things, perhaps, to be avoided. While Fischer (1978) suggests we may be moving (or have already substantially moved) to gerontofratria, I think that time is past. His book, *Growing Old in America*, sees a progress from gerontocracy (or headship of the old) through gerontophobia (fear of the old) to the current state of gerontofratria (brotherhood of the old or brotherhood with the old). We have, as I see it, swung back to gerontophobia, close enough to hating the old.

It is true that books about the pleasures of old age and how it can be successful abound. Movement looks to be toward a positive, esteemed image of the older adult. But, using the best interpretation, they are beacons on a darkening sea.

There are many negative signs on the horizon. Benefits to the elderly are being cut. Taxes on them are increasing. Take, for one example, Robert Butler's (1975) book, *Why Survive?* The title alone suggests problems, and reading it provides a litany of lament, a plethora of problems. Retirement is widely thought to be the harbinger of disease and death, though it is obviously not always that way (McCluskey and Borgatta 1981).

The life cycle poor are ghettoized in special locations, and buildings within those locations. Nursing home crises, replete with stories of difficulties, inadequate care, and even abuse, surface regularly. Even the better facilities seem devoid of meaning and purpose (Horner 1968; Tropman 1987).

A broad range of images of negativism and difficulty persist. Negative images, images which are held by "elders" as well as "youngsters," are discussed in Chapter 7. And very much like the material already mentioned about welfare, these images are ones which are directly contrary to the older respondent's own experience.

Life cycle poverty cannot be thought about in quite the same way as status poverty. It is not so much a question of whether one will become old or not, because the process of aging is inevitable. Rather, thinking about age may focus on avoiding life cycle poverty even though one grows old. That question I call the "quality-of-life" question.

The focus on quality is perhaps questionable. One can have a good life though old has a hollow ring. You cannot avoid it (as, it is thought, you can avoid status poverty) but it may not be so bad. Hence, control comes from thinking in ways that maintain quality control. It is not the condition itself that can be controlled, but, by a flip of the mind, the quality of that condition.

But there is an additional wrinkle to this argument, "entitlement," which links the old even more closely to the status poor. One almost has the sense of questioning whether one is entitled to a decent elderhood. It is somewhat as if one might have a positive or troubled aging life segment depending on whether one deserves it or not. It may be for this reason, in part, that researchers in the field of gerontology seem to literally be obsessed with questions about the quality of life in older ages, a topic of limited interest elsewhere. Chapter 8 considers these questions in the context of a national survey of older and younger people.[1]

Chapter 9 deals with some of the similarities between popular and scientific data. The popular and scientific comparison reveals more similarities than one might have thought, and some of the same continuities over the life cycle which have been observed elsewhere appear here. Some of the same misperceptions of older adults by older and younger adults alike (see the section on "Family Contact," for example) also surface.

Chapter 10 considers the policy opinion of older and younger adults from 1952 to 1978. It explores issues of conservatism in the older adult and shows that the image of seniors as conservative is generally false.

In conclusion, images of the life cycle poor serve the same purposes as images of the poor. Images of an overly bad older adulthood may serve a protective function, providing a psychological disengagement from aging (aging is bad; I'm well off, therefore I'm not aging) and protects the individual from having to deal with the more realistic aspects of this stage of the lifecourse.

It also, of course, tends to blame the victim for those who are not well off. By implication here, as well as with the poor, one can take comfort in the distancing which occurs in thinking "they," as opposed to "us," deserve what they get. But there may be aspects of cultural lag as well. In an era of higher death rates and no pensions or Social Security, old age doubtless had negative aspects. Even though the condition of the older adult is improved today, change in values and attitude may have lagged behind. The first stage of geronto-exploitation may not be far away. America as a society seeks resource-rich populations to tax.

NOTE

1. There are different approaches to entitlement justification. One, of course, is citizenship; another is, for seniors, the older and wiser status; still another is prior contributions. What one deserves always seems up for argument.

Chapter 7

Images of the Elderly

We have seen how attitudes toward the status poor exist seemingly independently of the conditions one might think would influence them. These negative images serve both as cause and effect: cause of actions toward the poor
and the effect of actions toward them. One might call it "reciprocal hatred."
We hate because we act; we act because we hate.

It is the purpose of this chapter to explore the attitudes and image of the
elders within American society.[1] Similar findings for the status poor emerge:
negativism and misperception, sustained in part by the victims themselves.

IMAGES OF THE ELDERLY: NEGATIVE INVERSION

The status poor have not always been hated. They were, for much of Western civilization, venerated. Ideas like *Pauperum Christi* (the Poor of Christ)
expressed the idea that the wealthy were the problem (and as likely to get into
the Kingdom of Heaven as through the eye of a needle). About the time of the
Reformation, one change that is not often mentioned was the change of the
status of the poor. Poverty became inverted. Poverty had been exalted; now it
was an occasion of sin. A similar shift, though much more recent, has affected the elderly. They too have experienced status inversion; they too have
moved from being loved to hated.

Achenbaum (1978), in his hallmark historical study, found both divergen-
cies and uniformities in views toward the elderly. Overall, he found the emer-

gence, early in society, of a veneration for the elderly as repositories of wisdom and examples of the well-lived life. After the Civil War, however, changes in this image created a developing disesteem, which continues to the present day and may be getting worse.

While there have been changes in the demographic and social conditions of the aged population, they do not seem to be directly related to the image of the elderly which was changing and evolving, negatively, over time. Achenbaum (1978, 86) comments, "Dramatic alterations in old people's actual place in American society have not always coincided with significant transformations in ideas about the elderly." He goes on to argue that disesteem arose before the change.

Continuities and change in the way Americans thought about elderly men and women before 1914 did not simply reflect shifts in the relation number of people over 60 in society, variation, in the population of older workers in the labor force, or alternatives in the perception and treatment of the aged poor. . . . The unprecedented denigration of older Americans arose independently of the most important observable changes in this actual status. (p. 86)

What has caused this attitude shift? It is a cultural change with unclear origins. Certainly, specific changes in social structure occurred. The advent of urbanization and industrialization which occurred after the Civil War and the changing roles associated with these shifts cannot be ignored. Roles change when transformations occur. When money became valued during the Reformation period, those without it became *ipso facto* unvalued. The last half of the nineteenth century was a time of great immigration. Those who came here were young, and had to reject home and parents/elders to make the trip. That rejection may have carried over. And perhaps other sources of information had something to do with it. People may have changed from personal exchange to a chief information source. In 1880 there were four books per hundred people, while in 1914 there were twelve per hundred, or a 200-percent increase.[2] Changes in family structure may have seperated immigrants and migrants from their elders, creating less exposure to seniors. Other sources and models of knowledge could also have affected the image of the aged quite apart from their physical numbers.[3] But like other cultural "facts" and changes in those facts, the image is somewhat independent of specific structural shifts. Let us see what seniors and others thought about themselves in 1978.

THE PALL OF PERCEPTION

Perhaps the most thorough set of survey attitudes were tapped by Louis Harris (1978) and his associates in their survey of *The Myth and Reality of Aging in America*. Generally, the crucial theme was that people attribute to the aged worse conditions than the aged actually report for themselves. But seniors themselves err in a negative direction.

Important as the idea of the view of people in general is, it is even more important to note that the elderly share the same stereotypes of the elderly that everyone else does. Here, too, there is a similarity to the attitudes toward the poor taken by the poor themselves. No one likes the poor, even those who are poor. Similarly, no one thinks the elderly are well off, even the elderly.

Life (Dis)Satisfaction

I performed my own analysis of the Harris data. Reported life satisfaction is a good place to start. Age is generally irrelevant to reported life satisfaction until one reaches the older ages (seventy-five and over) where it drops (see Table 7.1).

Old Age Looks Like Hell

Consider (see Tables 7.2 and 7.3) a contrast between people's perception of problems the elderly have and the problems both elderly and non-elderly report for themselves. The rankings within each column reverse themselves. People present the elderly as having more problems then the elderly actually have. The results are rather astonishing. About 31 percent of the respondents thought the elderly had many problems. On the other hand, in terms of actual problems experienced by respondents, 3.4 percent overall reported many problems, a number which ranged from 4.1 percent for those at age twenty-five to 1.4 percent for those over seventy-five. In other words, actual reported problems decreased with age, in complete contrast to the perception.

This result was similar to one found in thinking about the poor, as seen in Chapters 3 through 6. The attitudes are there, but they are relatively unaf-

Table 7.1
Life Satisfaction Scores by Age (Percentages)

Life Satisfaction	25 Years	25–34 Years	34–44 Years	45–54 Years	55–64 Years	65–74 Years	75+ Years	Totals
0 pts. (low)	0.0	0.2	0.0	0.0	0.0	0.1	0.1	0.1
1–12 points	4.8	3.9	5.0	7.6	5.7	8.2	10.5	5.9
12–24 points	26.2	25.1	22.2	27.1	33.4	31.5	39.5	27.7
25–36 points (high)	69.0	70.8	71.7	65.3	60.8	60.2	49.9	66.4
Totals	100.0	100.0	100.0	100.0	100.0	100.0	100.0	100.0

Source: L. Harris, *The myth and reality of aging in America* (Washington, D.C.: National Council on Aging, 1978)

Table 7.2
Image of Problems of the Elderly by Age Group

Imagined Problems	25 Years	25–34 Years	34–44 Years	45–54 Years	55–64 Years	65–74 Years	75+ Years	Totals
0 pts. (many problems)	34.3	30.1	29.9	30.2	31.4	30.5	27.3	30.9
1 point	22.7	18.8	17.0	15.5	14.8	21.1	18.2	18.3
2 points	16.0	18.1	15.2	16.1	14.3	14.7	17.7	16.1
3 points	10.2	14.0	12.9	16.9	12.7	10.7	12.8	13.1
4 points	8.6	6.1	12.4	6.2	7.6	7.9	7.2	8.0
5 points	2.1	2.7	3.2	4.9	5.1	5.1	5.3	3.7
6 points	2.0	3.1	2.8	3.4	2.8	2.9	4.3	2.9
7 points	2.2	1.4	2.0	3.1	3.5	2.4	3.0	2.4
8 points	1.9	1.6	2.9	3.1	3.5	2.4	3.0	2.4
9 points	0.0	2.9	0.8	0.9	1.3	1.4	0.7	1.2
10 points	0.0	0.4	0.5	1.0	3.1	0.6	0.8	0.9
11 points (hardly ever a problem)	0.0	0.7	0.4	0.9	0.7	0.7	0.1	0.5
TOTALS	100.0	100.0	100.0	100.0	100.0	100.0	100.0	100.0

Source: L. Harris, *The myth and reality of aging in America* (Washington, D.C.: National Council on Aging, 1978)

fected by the actual conditions in which the welfare directors find themselves. Similarly, in these data there is a negative perception of the later years which is not too affected by the demographic conditions of the respondents.

Even more astounding is that the attitudes are not much affected by the actual experiences of the elderly with old age. For example, Harris found that 30 percent of the respondents found the experience of old age better than expected. Many elderly, when reporting their own conditions, reported them better than they thought, or than they thought others thought. However, when asked about their general attitude, they appeared to disregard their own experience and share the more negative general perception.[4] The elderly appear to regard their own more positive experience as unique and not sufficient to change their own general view. In sum, the image of the elderly can be seen in the following ways:

1. Generally negative; full of problems and difficulties.

Table 7.3
Actual Problems of Elderly and Non-elderly by Age Categories

Actual Problems	25 Years	25–34 Years	34–44 Years	45–54 Years	55–64 Years	65–74 Years	75+ Years	Totals
0 points (many problems)	4.1%	3.8%	4.1%	3.3%	3.2%	1.9%	1.4%	3.4%
1 points	2.2	0.5	1.0	0.9	1.1	0.9	0.6	1.1%
2 points	0.4	1.5	0.8	0.8	1.9	1.3	1.5	1.0%
3 points	0.5	2.3	0.6	0.6	2.8	2.4	2.7	1.5%
4 points	2.9	2.2	3.6	1.7	2.7	3.1	3.5	2.7%
5 points	2.8	4.7	3.6	2.1	2.1	4.9	3.8	3.3%
6 points	5.6	5.4	1.4	2.7	4.3	5.4	6.9	4.3%
7 points	10.2	6.7	6.9	12.2	7.7	6.9	9.6	8.6%
8 points	11.7	11.6	11.3	9.3	11.0	11.7	10.8	11.1%
9 points	21.4	14.7	17.4	14.8	15.4	17.4	16.6	16.8%
10 points	17.1	21.1	23.0	23.6	21.6	21.6	22.2	21.3%
11 points (hardly ever a problem)	21.1	25.7	26.2	27.9	27.2	22.5	20.5	24.9
Totals	100.0	100.0	100.0	100.0	100.0	100.0	100.0	100.0

Source: L. Harris, *The myth and reality of aging in America* (Washington, D.C.: National Council on Aging, 1978)

2. There is little difference in this perception between those below sixty-five and those above, except those below are likely to see things a little more negatively than even those above do.

3. One's experiences, or one's demographic status (except race), does not cause much variation in people's opinion.

However, in terms of reports of actual conditions, the following is true:

1. Older people have, overall, about the same perceptions of actual problems as non-elderly.

2. Older people are less satisfied than young people only at the very highest levels of the scale.

The Magical Mystery of Myth

You might ask, though, if the different views can be explained. If one took standard demographic indicators—race, marital status, gender, health, education, and income levels—could the differences be accounted for? The answer is no. With respect to the image issue, actual conditions of life do not seem to explain the image of the aged for either non-aged (twenty-five to sixty-four) or aged (sixty-five and over). The total explained variance (R^2) is 2 to 4 percent. For actual problems, the ability to explain variance rises a bit to 33 to 38 percent, but is still low. However, life conditions do relate more to life problems than to the image of those problems. With respect to life satisfaction, life conditions do less to explain the life satisfaction of younger respondents ($R^2 = 18\%$) than the elders ($R^2 = 30\%$) (see Table 7.4).

Table 7.4
Image of the Aged, Actual Conditions Reported by the Aged and the Non-Aged, and Life Satisfaction Level of Aged and Non-Aged

	Non-Aged (25–64)	Aged (65+)
Image of the Aged[a]		
Mean Score	3.2	3.2
S.D.	2.4	2.3
Multiple R	.18	.15
R^2	.04	.02
Actual Problems[a]		
Mean Score	9.5	9.5
S.D.	2.5	2.5
Multiple R	.62	.57
R^2	.38	.33
Life Satisfaction[b]		
Mean Score	26.8	24.5
S.D.	6.9	7.8
Multiple R	.42	.54
R^2	.18	.30

[a]A multiple regression was run with six independent variables: race, marital status, gender, health, education, and income. The dependent variable for image was the extent to which eleven items were marked "hardly a problem" for the elderly by the respondents. For actual problems, the respondents used the same scale but referred to themselves and to actual conditions experienced by them, rather than things they thought would be a problem for the elderly. A score of 11 represents all eleven areas were "hardly a problem."

[b]The life satisfaction scale was calculated by Harris (1978, 156) and goes from 1 (low) to 36 (high).

CONCLUSION

The elderly and the non-elderly alike tend to see the older years as a time of troubles and problems. This view is not based on the elderly's actual experience with problems; nor is it based on social structural variables like income, race, and so on. The image of the aged is drawn from an as yet mysterious source of perceptions, perceptions which have the ability to motivate and generate action of a policy sort. These perceptions of the conditions of the elderly are, doubtless, a key factor in stimulating a pro-elderly federal social policy, but the shadow and gloom of negativity may be an important source of hatred of the life cycle poor.

I do not mean to suggest that seniors do not have problems. They do, something especially true of the older old and elderly of color. However, the perception of problems is, it appears, higher then their presence, even among those with personal experience. Perception becomes a kind of reality of its own.

NOTES

1. Support for the research in this chapter was provided, in part, by Grant #90-A-1325 of the Administration on Aging, for which appreciation is gratefully acknowledged. Special thanks go to Betty Sears for providing the data analysis.

2. Calculated by taking the number of books divided by the number of persons in the population, Table Series R-165-168/Table A1-3, pp. 499 and 7 respectively, *The Statistical History of the United States from Colonial Times to the Present* (New York: Horizon Press, 1965).

3. The ideas of freedom and equality, reinforced in the Civil War, are given high influence by David Fischer (1978), who sees disesteem beginning even earlier than Achenbaum.

4. This problem is not an uncommon one to radical organizers in any field. There needs to be the development of consciousness raising, of revolutionary consciousness, or some terms like that which point to a radical rethinking of the position the person occupies, and an important reevaluation of the evidence of his conditions which he typically considers. This change has occurred, if the *Better Homes and Gardens* data (Greer 1978) are to be believed, in the area of women's rights and men's duties (see Chapter 7). There, people report sharply changed perceptions of what is proper for men to do and report as well that these changed perceptions have changed their lives.

Chapter 8

American Culture and the Aged: Stereotypes and Realities

As already suggested, the stereotypes of old age generally run in a negative direction (see also Tibbitts 1979).[1] This negativism is contained in the very language we use to think and talk about older people. Phrases abound like "geezer," "coot," "old bag," and "old biddy."

One particularly egregious example is the myth of familial alienation—the disengagement idea—that seniors pull away from their families, perhaps as a preparation for death. This myth is not true and has not been true. Here is a case where negative stereotypes about seniors persist, and, phoenix-like, keep returning. Since the idea does not appear to have origins in fact, it must be that it serves some other purpose. I think it is sustained as a sort of rationale. The myth of alienation is a version, an expression, of "hate the poor." It is all right to hate the life cycle poor because they are pulling away anyway. I draw upon two sources of data to look at the relationship between myth and fact, much as I did in the last chapter, seeking to understand the nature of the "fact/value" separation and exploring the ways it might be used to provide fuel for poor hate.

The first of these is a Louis Harris poll (Harris 1978) of scientifically selected respondents whose views could be considered representative of both old and young people. The second is a self-selected popular survey, done through *Better Homes and Gardens* magazine in 1978 (Greer and Keating 1978).

The first point of interest was to see if there was much difference between senior and non-senior responses. In Chapter 7 those differences were minimal. Here we can look at further data, with similar results. The biggest gap was between values and attitudes and actuality, between what people believe and what is. This result requires us to look for functions of stereotypes and for the social purpose which such views sustain and fulfill. For example, it could be that stereotypes permit the undertaking of desired action when it is known (or could be known, anyway) that the available evidence would not support such action.[2]

Stereotypes may also be a way of communicating an unspoken message. Saying the life cycle poor are noncontributing may not really be the message. It may be that the person is saying, "Old people are not contributing anymore (and, unspoken) but I am and look at me. If you hate them (and if I hate them) you (I) cannot hate me (because of all I do)."

Thus, the speaker justifies his or her own position through "social contribution." Indeed, the main message of the stereotype may be in what is not said rather than what is said or whether the speaker is old or young. In this paradoxical sense, evidence that the stereotype is wrong may be too threatening to the message sender, because it has a negative impact on him or her. Thus, the message sender may redouble his or her efforts to reject the new information, to the dismay of the person with the correct scientific data. For example, if a well-off person agrees with the proposition that poor people are poor through luck and chance, his or her acceptance of that argument also means two things for him or her which are also unacceptable: (1) his or her own status is also due to luck and chance (depriving him or her of the opportunity to "own" his or her achievements) and (2) the permanence and certainty of his or her status can be questioned. If this hypothesis has merit, it suggests that older people who do contribute (in order to enhance respect) may miss the mark, since the real message may reflect the concerns about the speaker's own contribution, and evidence that the older person contributes may threaten, and lessen, his or her role.

Perhaps, then, hatred of the poor says more about the speaker than the victim. This idea, alluded to already, will be explored more in later sections.

DATA AND METHOD

As mentioned, the data here are drawn from two sources, a random scientific survey and a popular self-selected one. The former survey, completed by the Louis Harris Associates for the National Council on Aging (Harris 1978), will be known as the scientific or random sample. The other sample, the self-selected popular one, comes from a survey done through *Better Homes and Gardens* magazine (Greer and Keating 1978a, 1978b, 1977a, 1977b). In the scientific survey, Harris and associates interviewed 4,254 persons, with special sampling attention given to those over sixty-five. *Better Homes and Gardens* mailed out the same questionnaire in each of two issues of the magazine, and secured over 300 thousand responses. From this group, they selected a random sample of ten thousand; this smaller group forms the base of the analysis here. There is a three-year difference in the administration of the questionnaires; the scientific survey was done in 1975 and the popular one in 1978. This fact could account for some of the findings, and should be kept in mind, though it is probably not too significant. In addition, there are some differences in the age groupings, with the popular survey using age fifty-five as a dividing line and the scientific survey using sixty-five.[3]

PERSONAL VALUES

One area of interest is the realm of personal values. The *Better Homes and Gardens* (Greer and Keating 1978) survey contained questions directly related to this point. Table 8.1 reports the rankings (in terms of the proportion of people who responded "very important") respondents gave to a list of value-related items ranging from physical well-being to social status. Physical well-being was the most valued, with 86 percent of the respondents saying it was

Table 8.1
In Terms of Personal Success and Satisfaction How Important Is Each of These to You? (Percentage Responding "Very Important")

	Total	Under 35	35–54	55 and Over	Old/ Young	Old/ Middle
1. Physical well-being	86	86	87	85	−1	−2
2. Raising children	77	75	83	74	−1	−9
3. Intellectual growth	65	63	65	71	+8	+6
4. Spiritual growth	55	49	59	67	+18	+8
5. House/property	37	38	33	44	+6	+11
6. Financial achieve-ment/satisfaction	35	34	34	37	+3	+3
7. Job status/career	26	27	23	27	0	+4
8. Sexual attractiveness	22	27	18	15	−12	−3
9. Recognition by other	13	14	11	17	+3	+6
10. Influence on others	9	9	9	9	0	0
11. Social status	5	5	4	6	+1	+2
12. Other	7	7	7	5	−2	−2

Source: Calculated from data in G. G. Greer and K. Keating, "What's Happening to the American Family?" *Better Homes and Gardens*, 1978a.

Note: Multiple responses make Ns irrelevant.

very important; social status was at the low end, with 5 percent of the respondents saying it was very important. There is little or no difference by age within this table, overall. Since young, middle-aged, and older groups are presented, comparisons can be drawn between the old and the young and the old and the middle aged (see the last two columns of Table 8.1). The mean difference (disregarding sign) between the old and the young group is 4.6 percent; between the old and middle group it is also 4.6 percent. None of these differences merit much excitement, but there are some differences in the spiritual growth, house/property, and sexual attractiveness categories. Though there are some differences in proportion, the ranking is almost identical for all three groups; age does not, for the self-selected group, change the sense of preference or the priority of items.

And the order rankings are themselves of interest. Those who think that American society is crassly materialistic will be surprised to see the first four items—health, raising children, intellectual growth, and spiritual growth—are not among those which one would, perhaps, have thought. The great American dream of having a house does not come in until number five (especially interesting as the respondents are readers of *Better Homes and Gardens*), followed by financial and job achievements. Strikingly, in the age of sexual permissiveness, sexual attractiveness does not come in until number eight; it is followed by a group of "power" variables: recognition by others, influence over others, and social status. If one were to group them, it would be possible to summarize the first group as personal and family integrity and improvement followed by financial success, sex, and power.

Since this image diverges from popular understanding of what the American people seek, how can we understand it? The answer seems to be that the respondents were reporting what they felt they should feel, or even what they wished they could feel, instead of what they actually felt. And this image of what is "okay" to feel is broadly distributed through the ages.

SATISFACTION AND ACCOMPLISHMENT

Instructive, too, is an examination of issues pertaining to personal satisfaction and accomplishment. The *Better Homes and Gardens* (Greer and Keating 1978) study asked the respondents how satisfied they were with their progress toward realizing certain values or achieving certain goals (see Table 8.2). The ranking of progress toward goals is not the same as valuation of the goals themselves. Here, house and health tie for first place.[4] Sixty-nine percent of the respondents felt satisfied with the progress they had made or were making in these areas. Spiritual and intellectual growth, in third and fourth place in the valuation ranking, drop to and tie for ninth in the progress list.

Overall, there are not many differences among the age groups in terms of progress. Disregarding sign, there is an average difference of 4.9 percent between the old and the young, and 4.7 percent between the old and the middle

Table 8.2
Are You Satisfied with the Progress You Are Making toward Achieving These Goals? (Percentage Satisfied)

	Rank	Total	Under 35	35–54	55 and Over	Old/ Young	Old/ Middle
1. Physical well-being	1	69	70	68	65	−5	−3
2. Raising children	3	68	64	76	64	0	−12
3. Intellectual growth	9	57	57	57	57	0	0
4. Spiritual growth	9	57	55	59	59	+4	0
5. House/property	1	69	66	74	76	+10	+2
6. Financial achievement/ satisfaction	8	63	63	65	67	+4	+2
7. Job status/career	5	60	58	62	62	+4	0
8. Sexual attractiveness	4	63	65	63	54	−11	−9
9. Recognition by other	5	60	59	63	53	−6	−10
10. Influence on others	11	53	53	56	46	−7	−10
11. Social status	5	60	60	61	54	−6	−7
12. Other	12	4	4	4	2	−2	−2
Median		62	61	64	65		

Source: Calculated from data in G. G. Greer and K. Keating, "What's Happening to the American Family?" *Better Homes and Gardens*, 1978a.

groups. This difference is very close to the difference between the groups on the valuation list. What differences do exist seem to be in three areas: raising children, recognition by others, and influence over others. Close behind are sexual attractiveness and social status.

Thus, in the popular survey there is little difference on the questions of life values and progress toward achieving goals related to those values. An exception is that older people see themselves as somewhat less attractive and powerful than their younger counterparts. In terms of a hate-the-poor culture, a situation where the victims believe themselves to be less attractive and having less prestige than the majority culture is exactly where you would want them.

HOW IS YOUR LIFE WORKING OUT?

The Harris poll (1978) had a question on "Your life, now, compared to what you expected it to be when you were younger." That question, though much less specific, is similar to the "progress" question in the popular survey (see Table 8.3). Here, too, there is minimal difference among the age groups,

Table 8.3
Your Life Now Compared to What You Expected It to Be (in 1975) When You Were Younger? (Percentages)

	18–64	18–35	36–54	55–64	65+
Better than expected	37	37.4	39.7	26.9	31.9
Worse than expected	11	12.8	8.8	11.3	10.8
About the way expected	47	45.2	46.9	55.2	47.3
Not sure	5	4.6	4.5	6.7	10.0
Total	100	100.0	99.9	100.1	100.0

Source: Calculated from data in L. Harris, *The myth and reality of aging in America* (Washington, D.C., National Council on Aging, 1978), 111.

with one exception: The fifty-five to sixty-four age group felt less than any of the other groups that their lives worked out better than expected.

Of the entire eighteen to sixty-four age group, 37 percent found life better than they had expected it, as did 32 percent of the over sixty-five group. The same proportion (47%) of the younger and older groups found things "about the way they expected it." More older people were unsure than younger people: 10 percent as compared to 5 percent. Considering the fact that there is an age span of more than sixty years (from people eighteen to those over eighty), this consistency is quite remarkable. Moreover, the better/worse ratio is in the vicinity of three to one.

MANDATORY RETIREMENT

One can look at mandatory retirement in several ways. One way is that it provides a well-deserved rest for society's contributors, a rest provisioned by Social Security benefits and private pensions. Another way is that it interdicts choice. A third way is that everyone should work; seniors are no more exempt than anyone else. In the mid-1970s, almost no one wanted mandatory retirement. Over 80 percent of the respondents in both surveys were against it (see Tables 8.4 and 8.5).

THE FORGOTTEN SENIORS

Family contact is one of the areas where there is perhaps the most mythology about older people, specifically that they are abandoned and alone. This point is of great concern to those in the field of aging. What does the *Better Homes and Gardens* (Greer and Keating 1978) survey say about family relations?

Table 8.4
Should There Be Mandatory Retirement at Age 65? (Percentages)

	Total	Under 35	35–54	55 and Over
Yes	15	12	17	19
No	83	87	81	79
Did not answer	2	1	2	2

Source: Calculated from data in G. G. Greer and K. Keating, "What's Happening to the American Family?" *Better Homes and Gardens*, 1978a, p. 114.

Table 8.5
Agree (Strongly or Somewhat) with Statements about Retirement (1975, Percentages)

	Total	Under 35	35–54	55–64	65+
Nobody should be forced to retire because of age, if he wants to continue working and is still able to do a good job	84.5	87.9	87.2	82.6	84.5

Source: Calculated from data in L. Harris, *The myth and reality of aging in America* (Washington, D.C., National Council on Aging, 1978), 216.

Respondents were asked whether they thought the elderly are forgotten by their families. The overwhelming majority (72%; Table 8.6) think the aged are forgotten, with somewhat higher proportions of younger people, as opposed to older people, believing this. Still, a substantial 66 percent of the older group think that the elderly are forgotten by their families. The myth, *qua* myth, is true.

CONTACT WITH FRIENDS AND FAMILY

But how does what people think relate to what people do? Respondents (those who have relatives and close friends) were asked whether they had seen friends or relatives within certain recent periods of time: the last day, the last week or two, or a month or more ago.[5] There may be some inflation here: Parents report seeing children more than children report seeing parents, grandparents report seeing grandchildren more than grandchildren report seeing grandparents, and so on.

Table 8.6
Do You Think the Elderly Are Forgotten by Families? (Percentages)

	Total	Under 35	35–54	55 and Over
Yes	72	75	70	66
No	27	24	29	31
No Answer	2	1	1	3

Source: Calculated from data in G. G. Greer and K. Keating, "What's Happening to the American Family?" *Better Homes and Gardens*, 1978a.

Specifically, of those over sixty-five, 49 percent had seen their children within the last day or so, and 25 percent had seen them within the last two weeks (see Table 8.7). Twenty-five percent had not seen their children for a month or more. These data do not suggest that older folks are forgotten. It just seems that way, or perhaps we would like it to be that way.

For almost everyone (except parents seeing their children), friends are the largest source of daily contact. Older people were even more likely to have seen close friends, 59 percent within a day or two and 31 percent within the last day or two. Only 9 percent had not seen close friends for a month or more.

WHO SHOULD TAKE CARE OF MOTHER?

If an aging parent can no longer live alone, where might the best place for him or her be? Two alternatives—in a nursing home or with children—are addressed by the *Better Homes and Gardens* (Greer and Keating 1978b) material (see Table 8.8). As a testimony to ambivalence, the respondents split exactly in half, with 47 percent going to each alternative.

ARE ELDERS USEFUL ANYMORE?

American society likes you better if you make an effort. Everyone ought to "chip in." The perceptions about the "usefulness" of older people might tell us a lot. Harris (1978) asked about this point, and the results are instructive (see Table 8.9). Of the total public, only 23 percent saw "most people over 65" as "very useful," but 69 percent reported responses of "somewhat useful/ not sure." There is a 9 percent difference between the elderly and the non-elderly, with the elderly more likely to see their age group as very useful.

Table 8.7
Contact (Seen) with Friends and Family (1975 Percentages)

	Have	Seen within Last Day or So (Includes Live With)	Seen within Last Day or Two	Seen a Month or More Ago	Total Base for Each Cell
Close Friends, Median		**60.5**	**32.6**	**6.5**	
Under 35	96.7	62.2	27.3	6.5	100.0
35–54	88.2	60.3	32.8	6.4	99.5*
55–64	95.1	60.7	32.3	6.9	99.8*
65+	95.0	59.4	30.7	9.5	99.5*†
Children, Median		**59.4**	**13.8**	**27.2**	
Under 35	52.7	67.7	2.7	29.6	100.0
35–54	90.9	63.7	7.2	29.2	100.0
55–64	89.3	55.2	20.5	24.2	100.0
65+	80.6	49.3	25.5	25.1	99.9*†
Brothers & Sisters, Median		**19.6**	**29.8**	**48**	
Under 35	94.5	35.9	27.6	36.5	100.0
35–54	87.8	18.4	31.9	49.7	100.0
55–64	88.8	18.9	34.3	46.3	99.5*
65+	79.1	20.3	21.8	57.3	99.6*†
Parents, Median		**32.1**	**26.6**	**37.5**	
Under 35	89.0	43.0	21.4	35.5	100.0
35–54	65.4	32.1	28.5	39.4	100.0
55–64	21.8	32.1	31.1	36.8	100.0
65+	4.0	29.7	22.0	47.2	98.9*†
Grandchildren					
65+	75.1	42.8	28.4	28.5	99.7*†
Grandparents, Median		**20.8**	**20.1**	**58.4**	
Under 35	54.5	20.8	21.2	58.0	100.0
35–54	11.3	9.7	13.9	76.4	100.0
55–64	1.6	42.2	20.1	37.7	100.0

Source: Calculated from data in L. Harris, *The myth and reality of aging in America* (Washington, D.C., National Council on Aging, 1978), 166.

Note: Each cell value calculated on 100 percent. Thus, 96.7 percent of under-35 respondents listed in row 1 have close friends, 67.2 percent have seen them within the last day or so, and so on.

*Other percent age "not sure."

†Indicates the places where our analysis produced slightly different (2–5%) results from the published Harris results; in each instance the Harris proportions were higher in the first column.

Table 8.8
Where Is the Best Place for Aging Parents No Longer Capable of Living Alone? (Percentages)

	Total	Under 35	35–54	55+
Retirement or nursing home	47	44	47	59
With their children	47	50	46	35
Did not answer	6	6	7	6

Source: Calculated from data in G. G. Greer and K. Keating, "What's Happening to the American Family?" *Better Homes and Gardens*, 1978a.

Table 8.9
Image of "Most People Over 65" as Useful Members of the Community (1975 Percentages)

	Very Useful	Somewhat Useful; Not Sure	Not Useful at All	Total
Total Public	23.0	69.0	8.0	100.0
Under 35	21.1	70.1	8.7	99.9
35–54	20.6	71.9	7.4	99.8
55–64	24.3	68.1	7.4	99.8
65+	31.6	61.7	6.6	99.8

Source: Calculated from data in L. Harris, *The myth and reality of aging in America* (Washington, D.C., National Council on Aging, 1978), 64.

RESPECT

Central to the notion of hate is the notion of nonrespect. As Wolfensberger (1972) pointed out, lack of respect is one of the key elements of hate. If the elderly are hated, they should get "no respect" (see Table 8.10). Here is one of the most interesting data sets.

More than 70 percent of the young and young middle-aged people felt that the elderly got too little respect. No doubt the respondents were talking about what they felt. On the other hand, as is sometimes the case with victims of "isms" (sexism, classism, racism, etc.), the seniors in 1975 did not think things were so bad. Their 44-percent response in that category is in sharp contrast. Confirming this trend is the lower percentage of younger people as compared

Table 8.10
Whether People over Sixty-Five Get the Right Amount of Respect from Younger People These Days (1975 Percentages)

	Under 35	35–54	55–64	65+	Median
Too much respect	0.4	1.2	0.4	0.7	0.6
Too little respect	75.4	72.7	54.9	43.9	63.8
Just the right amount	18.0	19.3	34.5	39.2	18.8
It depends (volunteered)	3.3	4.3	7.1	10.9	5.7
Not sure	2.9	2.5	3.1	5.4	2.8
Total	100.0	100.0	100.0	100.0	

Source: Calculated from data in L. Harris, *The myth and reality of aging in America* (Washington, D.C., National Council on Aging, 1978), 66.

to older people who thought the elderly got "just the right amount" of respect (18% as opposed to 39%).

WHAT THESE RESULTS SUGGEST
IN TERMS OF POOR HATE

Let us take a look at these patterns overall:

Satisfaction and Accomplishment—similar findings across ages; physical health first, children second, and social status last.

How Is Your Life Working Out—similar across ages; 60 percent median satisfaction; health first.

Mandatory Retirement—all agree it should be eliminated.

The Forgotten Elderly—overall, 72 percent think the elderly are forgotten by families; 66 percent of seniors think so.

Contact with Friends and Family—friends and children are important: about 60 percent of the respondents had seen them in the last day or so, grandchildren come next (42.8%), parents follow at 32 percent, and brothers and sisters bring up rear (19.6%).

Who Should Take Care of Mother—split; 47 percent each say children and nursing home.

Are the Elderly Useful Anymore—overall, only 23 percent say very useful (31% of seniors).

Respect—a substantial 63.8 percent think the elderly get too little respect (75% of those under thirty-five think so, as opposed to 44% of seniors).

One way to look at these findings is to emphasize the similarity. And there are many similarities: in things that are important, in overall sense of accomplishment, in opposing mandatory retirement, and so on. But no one says you cannot hate people similar to you.

Other findings intimate a more ominous twist. A 61-percent satisfaction rate with accomplishment is, in academic terms, a failing grade. One could well imagine younger people seeing elders as in the way of their accomplishment. For one thing, they are not much use anymore (suggesting potential need for care). When a senior cannot care for himself or herself there was a split on whether a nursing home or a relative's home was better. Everyone thought the elderly should at least be able to work (no more mandatory retirement). Elders were thought to get little respect, and the myth of familial alienation persisted in spite of frequent contact.

CONCLUSION

There is plenty of ammunition here for hate. No one said hate—they were not asked. It is a kind of stereotype. What we see, then, is negative stereotypes generated in the face of actual differences. Several factors which are related to stereotypes and how stereotypic images are maintained might help explain the differences between the image of the aged and their actual situations, as well as the differences between younger and older respondents.

First, stereotypes may serve to replace critical thought where thought is difficult or painful or where evidence is lacking or hard to evaluate. All of these conditions may apply in the area of intergenerational relationships. Each generation may not want to take the time to find out about the other, or the process of finding out may be a difficult and sensitive one. If many people experience this kind of tension in relating to people of different ages, then substituting stereotypical images of real relationships may well serve to reduce the tension. Stereotypes are "functional" in this sense, and serve the practical purpose of reducing complex situations to simplistic, dichotomous ones.

Another function stereotypes might have is to provide information of a certain sort where correct information is lacking. But suppose that accurate information is available but is rejected. One needs to ask, therefore, why certain information percolates well through the public mind and other information does not seem to take hold at all.

We would answer in part by saying that we need many of our stereotypes. They serve us both well and poorly. They protect us from our own inadequacies. If we believe that older people are largely forgotten by their families, then the attention that we pay to the elderly of our own families will seem more adequate, if not magnanimous. Similarly, if older people believe that others are worse off than they in this regard, they will feel better about themselves and their relatives. After all, it must be difficult to admit to oneself that one's family cares too little and forgets too much.

Stereotypes about older people—as in the case of other groups, such as Blacks and women—allow us to treat the elderly as less than fully human. As a result, we might proceed to strip older people of jobs, financial power, status, and even civil rights with less guilt than we otherwise might feel.

NOTES

1. I want to thank Carol Hollenshead, Director of the Center for the Education of Women at the University of Michigan, for her work on an early version of this material.

2. Conversely, lack of action can also be rationalized. An example is the idea that victims of crime, young or old, deserved what they got because they were, in some way, careless or did something that invited the action. If we hold this view, then it does not become necessary for us to compensate victims.

3. As a partial recompense, the Harris data were recalculated, permitting us to see a more detailed age breakdown than was given in the published version.

4. This ranking occurs even as the percentage of chronic illness increases. However, reference group considerations are important here.

5. Recent in this context is related to the time the question was asked, in 1976.

Chapter 9

What the Public Thinks:
Older and Younger Adults

As a final effort to review what the elderly and non-elderly think, a focus on public opinion is useful. What do the elderly think, and how different is it from what younger citizens think? In particular, given the important role of government in the lives of the elderly during the last thirty years or so, exploration of what older and younger respondents thought about the role and function of government could be revealing. Further attention might be paid to the important issue of civil rights, as well as to those areas of "traditional" concerns such as work, family, and church attendance. Three general questions guide these analyses:

1. Have values changed over the last thirty years?
2. What is the relationship of the elderly to the non-elderly with respect to such change or constancy as has occurred?
3. What do the findings mean in terms of policy? What has been going on in policy arenas which relates to, or does not relate to, the value system?

DATA AND METHOD

The primary source of data was the American National Election Studies (NES) stored at the Inter-University Consortium for Political and Social Research at the University of Michigan. The NES have been conducted every two years since 1952, with minor studies in 1948, 1951, 1953, 1954, and

1960. Because the studies have been conducted for nearly thirty years, and because their validity has been the object of much additional research, we have confidence in the overall quality of the NES data. In addition, the data are consistent over a period of years, permitting construction of a longitudinal baseline of analysis. The data here run between 1958 and 1978.

Other data include Gallup and Harris public opinion polls. The polls provided a number of useful questions, but the questions were less consistent and less uniform over the years than the NES questions. The data are presented using percentages.

ECLIPSE OF PUBLIC FUNCTION

Public opinion is a lot like what was once called "common sense," when common sense meant a view that was held in common by a variety of different people. Indeed, the fact that common sense guides people in their opinions on issues is a basic principle of democracy itself. One important finding from these analysis was the increasing distrust of government.

Trust In Government

No democratic government can operate without the consent of the governed (Tropman 1987, 187). How that consent evolves and how the government and others go about engineering that consent are major elements in the political system. In America, there has been a substantial loss of trust in government over recent decades. Between 1958 and 1978, a span of twenty years, the percentage of Americans who had confidence in the ability of the government in Washington to do what is right just about always or most of the time fell from 73 to 30 percent (see Table 9.1).

The elderly's view was similar to that of the young, though the elderly were somewhat more distrustful. In each survey from 1958 through 1978, those sixty-five and over were the least trusting among the three age groups. In 1958, 63 percent of them said they trusted the government in Washington just about always or most of the time, but only 24 percent said this in 1978. The percentage of those with high trust—those who think the government always does what is right—slipped from 15 percent in 1958 to 5 percent in 1978. The spread between the oldest and youngest groups has remained about the same over the period, approximately 10 percent.

It is fascinating to consider why this eclipse of trust in government has occurred at the very time when government activities have shown unusually rapid growth in areas concerning the elderly. One explanation for this paradox could be that the very growth in government itself has caused people to be more critical of its activities. As the government does more, it makes itself more vulnerable to criticism.

Table 9.1
Trust in Government (Percentages)

	Age	1958	1964	1966	1968	1970	1972	1974	1976	1978
All Respondents										
Always		16	14	17	7	7	7	3	3	3
Most of the Time		57	62	48	54	47	48	34	30	27
Depends		—	—	1	—	—	—	—	—	—
Some of the Time		23	22	28	36	44	44	61	62	64
Never		7	0	3	0	1	0	1	2	4
Don't Know		4	2	3	2	2	2	2	3	3
Total		100	100	100	99	101	101	101	100	101
By Age										
Always	Under 30	19	17	20	7	6	6	4	4	2
	30–64	15	14	16	8	7	5	2	3	2
	Over 65	15	12	16	7	6	4	3	3	5
Most of	Under 30	59	65	51	63	52	50	39	34	31
the Time	30–64	59	63	49	54	48	48	33	30	27
	Over 65	48	59	42	44	39	42	25	25	19
Depends	Under 30	—	—	2	29	—	—	—	—	—
	30–64	—	—	1	36	—	—	—	—	—
	Over 65	—	—	2	45	—	—	—	—	—
Some of	Under 30	20	18	22	—	40	41	55	61	62
the Time	30–64	23	22	29	—	44	45	64	63	64
	Over 65	30	25	31	—	51	49	60	62	67
Never	Under 30	—	—	1	—	—	1	0	0	4
	30–64	—	—	3	—	—	0	0	1	4
	Over 65	—	—	3	—	—	1	2	0	2
Don't Know	Under 30	3	0	4	1	2	2	2	1	2
	30–64	3	1	2	2	1	2	1	3	3
	Over 65	7	5	6	4	5	4	6	10	7
Total	Under 30	101	100	100	100	100	100	100	100	101
	30–64	100	100	100	100	100	100	100	100	100
	Over 65	100	101	100	100	100	100	100	100	100

Governmental Benefit

One specific reason for low trust reflected in the polls is that people feel that government is not working for them, or being responsive to them (Tropman 1987, 188). Instead, it may seem that the government is primarily working for the benefit of others. The public opinion question that elicits this response asks, "Would you say the government is pretty much run by a few big interests looking out for themselves or that it is run for the benefit of all the people?" Here, too, the data are quite revealing (see Table 9.2). Since 1964, the viewpoint that the government is run by a few big interests has been receiving more and more support among all three age groups, rising from 29 percent in 1964 to 72 percent in 1978. The opinions of the elderly have presaged those of younger age groups. In 1964, only 57 percent of the elderly felt that government was run for the benefit of all, compared to 70 percent of those under thirty. In 1968, 43 percent of the sixty-five-and-over group felt that the government was run for the benefit of all, compared to 56 percent of the under-thirty group. By 1978, only 21 percent of the sixty-five-and-over group responded that the government was run for the benefit of all, in comparison with the still higher 26 percent of the under-thirty group.[1]

The pattern by age group reflects greater doubt on the part of elders, as compared to those of younger ages, at every measurement period. However, this may be due to a cohort rather than to an aging effect, because the gap between the two groups gradually narrows over the years.

Is the Government Too Powerful?

Perhaps the best way to sum up the indicators used here is to focus on the significance in American political history of the controversy over the limits of government power that have pervaded our political system from the Pilgrims right through to the protesters (Tropman 1987, 194). During this century, this issue of government power emerged forcefully during the Great Depression and World War II, when a rushing stream of privatism was disrupted by massive government action. The next period of large-scale government activity took place during the 1960s. The controversy over the appropriate degree of government power is reflected in the fluctuations since 1964 in public opinion about the issue. In 1964, 30 percent of the populace thought the government in Washington was getting too powerful, "for the good of the country and the individual person." This proportion rose to 41 percent in 1968, dropped to 31 percent in 1970, rose to 49 percent in 1976, and dropped to 43 percent in 1978. The counterview that "the government has not gotten too strong" ran around 30 percent until 1976, when the percentage having this sentiment dropped to 20 percent and then to 14 percent in 1978 (see Table 9.3).

The age group distribution is quite interesting. In 1966, a substantially larger group of elders (48%) than of younger people thought the government

Table 9.2
Who Is the Government Run for the Benefit Of? (Percentages)

	Age	1958	1964	1966	1968	1970	1972	1974	1976	1978
All Respondents										
Give Everyone a Break*		18	64	53	51	41	38	25	24	24
Pro–Con Depends		1	4	6	5	3	2	2	2	1
Few Big Interests		76	29	33	40	50	53	66	66	67
Don't Know		5	4	7	5	4	7	7	7	8
Total		100	101	99	101	100	101	100	99	100
By Age										
Give	Under 30	16	70	61	56	50	39	30	25	26
Everyone	30–64	18	64	54	52	41	38	24	24	25
a Break*	Over 65	20	57	42	43	30	36	20	23	21
Pro–Con	Under 30	1	3	5	7	5	2	3	2	1
Depends	30–64	1	5	7	5	6	3	3	3	1
	Over 65	0	2	6	3	4	2	1	2	1
Few Big	Under 30	79	24	28	35	43	54	61	68	64
Interests	30–64	77	29	33	39	50	53	68	67	67
	Over 65	71	33	41	47	59	53	68	63	68
Don't Know	Under 30	3	2	7	2	3	5	7	5	9
	30–64	5	3	6	5	3	6	5	6	7
	Over 65	10	8	12	7	8	9	11	13	11
Total	Under 30	99	99	101	100	101	100	101	100	100
	30–64	101	101	100	101	100	100	100	100	100
	Over 65	101	100	101	100	101	100	100	100	100

*In 1958, the answer was "For the benefit of all."

in Washington was too powerful. In 1968, however, this proportion dropped radically, to 35 percent, and has not varied substantially since. What might account for this crossover in opinion about government power among the elderly?

The beginnings of political action on behalf of the elderly in the early 1960s culminating in the enactment of Medicare and the Older Americans Act in 1965 may have placed the government in a new light for older people. Not the benevolent or paternalistic provider of social services it once was, the government may have begun to be seen as the avuncular controller of important resources which, like the person who guides one's trust fund at the bank, does not always agree to let one have what one wants in all instances. How-

Table 9.3
Is the Government in Washington Getting Too Powerful?

	Age	1964	1966	1968	1970	1972	1976	1978
All Respondents								
The government is getting too powerful		30	39	41	31	41	49	43
Other; depends		3	4	3	6	4	3	2
The government is not getting too powerful		36	27	30	33	27	20	14
Don't know; no opinion		31	31	27	30	28	28	42
Total		100	101	101	100	100	100	101
By Age								
The government	Under 30	26	35	40	25	41	47	37
is getting	30–64	31	37	42	33	42	54	46
too powerful	Over 65	33	48	35	31	38	40	42
Other;	Under 30	5	6	5	8	5	4	2
depends	30–64	3	3	2	5	3	3	1
	Over 65	2	1	2	5	3	1	2
The government	Under 30	38	29	28	37	25	20	13
is not getting	30–64	35	29	31	34	28	20	14
too powerful	Over 65	36	16	30	28	28	19	15
Don't know;	Under 30	32	29	27	31	29	29	48
no opinion	30–64	31	30	25	28	27	24	39
	Over 65	30	35	33	37	31	40	42
Total	Under 30	101	99	100	101	100	100	100
	30–64	100	99	100	100	100	100	100
	Over 65	101	100	100	101	100	100	101

ever, once the benefits of these laws began to be felt during the late 1960s and early 1970s, it is possible that older people began to feel more positively toward the government.

My sense is that the elderly remained consistent in their views, if consistency is seen as slow movement with the general tide, and the younger age groups changed more rapidly in theirs. Thus, rather than seeing the politics of protection—with the elderly having achieved substantial benefits through government action in social services and medical care—now closing the door to others, we see the politics of disenchantment, with citizens of all ages becoming annoyed at the government's actions and withdrawing approval.

RIGHTING CIVIL WRONGS

American society is built on the proposition of liberty and justice for all. Equality and fair play have been our hallmark. On the other hand, as Myrdal (1944, 1962) has observed, we have an "American dilemma." Despite our having carved out numerous institutions to serve these ideals, groups such as Blacks, women, the disabled, and the elderly still suffer discrimination and isolation. Slavery was a mark against American culture; its demise has not ended poor treatment of minorities. Rather, as slavery came to a close, discrimination began, and was legitimated by the Supreme Court's separate-but-equal decision (*Plessey v. Ferguson*, 163 U.S. 537 [1896]). It was not until almost the middle of this century, with the outlawing of restrictive covenants in property deeds (*Shelley v. Kraemer*, 334 U.S. 1 [1948]), that some progress was made. Harry Truman desegregated the armed forces, and, in 1954, *Brown v. Topeka Board of Education* (347 U.S. 483 [1954]; 349 U.S. 294 [1955]) continued the struggle to achieve full equality. Then, in the 1960s, American society experienced the full force of the civil rights revolution, with those whose rights had been denied, abrogated, or curtailed coming forward. Along with their supporters, they used other rights legally granted by our political system to make their plight known and to demand redress.

American society is riddled with "isms"—ageism, racism, sexism—in which people are judged not by their capabilities but by some other ascriptive features of their person not relevant to any pertinent judgment. Only through the constant vigilance of those who suffer discrimination is progress made, and even then it is slow. Even as Americans believe that these people are entitled to the same rights as other Americans, they also insist that those who want rights fulfilled must fight for them and earn them by their own efforts. Some help may be acceptable, but help from government sources is apparently legitimate only if it is matched with some effort by the aggrieved.

The Speed of Civil Rights

In 1964, the National Election Study began a series of questions on American's perception of the appropriate speed of the civil rights movement: "Do you think that civil rights leaders are trying to push too fast, are going too slowly, or are they moving about the right speed?" In this particular case, the question has remained the same throughout the administration of the item, so that there are no problems of question comparability. But problems do arise in trying to interpret the meaning of the responses (Tropman 1987, 196). Between 1964 and 1976 (the question was not asked in 1978), the proportion of people who responded that the "civil rights people have been trying to push too fast" dropped from 63 to 39 percent. Correspondingly, the proportion of those who thought that the progress was "about right" increased from

25 to 47 percent in that period. The proportion of "don't knows" remained essentially stable (see Table 9.4).

The growing belief that progress in civil rights activities is about right can be interpreted in a variety of ways. One interpretation of these changes could be that there has been a growing acceptance of civil rights activity. Alternatively, it could be argued that the civil rights movement has slowed down over the last decade so the trend represents a growing conservatism in the 1970s. The responses may indicate that people are glad that civil rights activities have slowed down. Our interpretation lies between these two perspectives.

The 1960s not only brought advances in entitlements, but also forms of struggle that the public thought inappropriate: riots and some of the more militant episodes in the civil rights movement. Though the civil rights question may have been intended to focus on the rights of Blacks, the public is prone to associate a variety of protest activities with civil rights, so that the question may also in part have tapped public sentiment about the rights of draft resisters, Vietnam protesters, and other activists. This may explain why the public believed that the civil rights people were pushing too fast during the 1960s. As they have become accustomed to or more tolerant of these activities, or as these activities have decreased, their support for civil rights activities has increased.

On the other hand, the public often tends to react against change of any kind. It is likely that some will regard change, even in a direction of which they approve, as "going too fast." Therefore, the decline in the proportion of people who think things are going too fast may reflect an overall perception that there has been a slower pace of change, rather than a greater acceptance of civil rights activities.

The range of age group differences is minimal. The elderly showed no consistent pattern of response here. Sometimes they were slightly less likely than younger age groups to think that the pace of change was too fast (1964, 1968); at other times they were slightly more likely to have this sentiment (1966, 1972, 1976). Age functions here chiefly as a marginal modifier, and not as a vigorous or consistent one. All three age groups responded similarly. Increasingly, all three groups tended to respond more favorably toward the speed of the civil rights movement. As mentioned, it is very difficult to interpret this trend. It depends on whether people perceive the rate of the civil rights movement as essentially the same or as slower. If they perceive the rate as essentially the same, then their responses reflect a growing acceptance of civil rights activities. If they perceive the rate as slower, then their responses reflect that attitudes toward civil rights have not changed.

One conclusion that can be drawn from the similarity of responses among all three age groups is that older people are not more likely to identify with Blacks than younger people, an assumption which is often made. Even though people enter into a minority status upon reaching the age of sixty-five, they do not immediately or automatically begin to identify with minority groups. But they may feel or sense oppression and threat. Even if you do not call

Table 9.4
Public Attitudes towards the Speed of the Civil Rights Movement

	Age	1964	1966	1968	1972	1976
All Respondents						
Too fast; somewhat too fast		63	65	63	46	39
Depends		—	—	—	—	—
About right		25	19	28	41	47
Too slow; somewhat too slow		5	5	7	8	8
Don't know		6	11	3	5	5
Total		99	100	101	100	99
By age						
Too fast;	Under 30	63	62	59	39	34
somewhat too fast	30–64	64	65	65	49	41
	Over 65	61	67	57	47	43
Depends	Under 30	—	1	—	—	—
	30–64	—	1	—	—	—
	Over 65	—	0	—	—	—
About right	Under 30	24	22	29	45	51
	30–64	26	20	28	40	46
	Over 65	24	13	26	39	44
Too slow;	Under 30	8	8	10	13	11
somewhat	30–64	5	4	5	7	8
too slow	Over 65	5	3	8	5	5
Don't know	Under 30	5	7	2	3	4
	30–64	6	10	2	4	5
	Over 65	10	17	8	9	9
Total	Under 30	100	100	100	100	100
	30–64	101	100	100	100	100
	Over 65	100	100	99	100	101

the American Association of Retired Persons (AARP), they will call you. Even if you do not ask for the senior discount, clerks may ask you if you want it. There may be the queasy sense that you have changed in the eyes of others, even if not in your own.

Women's Roles

Beginning in 1972, a question was asked by the National Election Study on attitudes toward women's rights. Respondents were asked to indicate whether they thought women should have equal roles with men, or whether "a woman's place is in the home" (see Table 9.5).

Within the recent past, the overall distribution of responses has been quite consistent. About 50 percent of the respondents have felt that women should have an equal role (though it does increase to 57% in 1978). The proportion of persons who thought that women should remain in the home dropped from 29 percent in 1972 to 21 percent in 1978. A substantial proportion of respondents were neutral, about 16 percent. The distribution of responses on this question aptly illustrates the conflicting attitudes of the American populace. In a land where "all men are created equal," and after more than a decade of vigorous effort to bring to the attention of the public the problems of women, only about 50 percent of the population was willing to accord them an equal role to men.

Because the age group effect is so striking, it is essential to take a generational perspective on the results here. Younger cohorts, those under thirty, have been in favor of an equal role for women to the tune of 55 to 67 percent. The middle-age group is sharply below that percentage, and the oldest age group is slightly lower still. Only slightly more than one-third of those sixty-five and over support an equal role for women, despite the fact that there are 130 women for every 100 men sixty-five and older, and the gap widens with increasing age. The oldest age group also shows a larger proportion of "no opinion" and "don't know" responses. Clearly, there is a generational thrust apparent in the responses of the elderly, but it is one heavily mixed with ambivalence.

Rights of the Accused

The data on rights of the accused, as with the roles of women, covers only a short span of time, from 1970 to 1978. The question asks whether we should do "everything possible" to protect the legal rights of the accused, or is it "more important to stop criminal activity even at the risk of reducing the rights of the accused?" (see Table 9.6) (Tropman 1987, 198). The overall proportions of responses are arresting. About 29 percent of the respondents felt that the rights of the accused should be protected. A higher proportion, in the vicinity of 40 to 46 percent (except for 1974), felt that crime should be stopped even at the expense of reducing those rights. Elderly respondents tended to distribute themselves into the "stop crime" and the "don't know" categories, particularly the "stop crime" category. An average of 47 percent of the elderly felt that crime should be stopped even at the risk of reducing the rights of the accused.

It is important to emphasize the high proportion of the "don't know" responses here (for everyone, but higher for elderly). Whether these responses are a way of remaining neutral or whether they represent more complex feelings is hard to determine. We are inclined to think that they represent a refuge to which people retreat either when they are pressed too hard to take a posi-

Table 9.5
Public Attitudes towards Women's Rights

	Age	1972	1974	1976	1978
All Respondents					
Women should have equal rights		46	50	50	57
Neutral		19	18	18	16
Women's place is in the home		29	26	23	21
Don't know; no opinion		5	6	9	6
Total		99	100	100	100
By age					
Women should	Under 30	55	66	61	67
have equal rights	30–64	45	46	51	56
	Over 65	37	38	33	40
Neutral	Under 30	18	15	18	16
	30–64	21	20	17	17
	Over 65	17	17	20	17
Women's place	Under 30	24	16	16	14
is in the home	30–64	30	29	24	22
	Over 65	34	34	31	35
Don't know;	Under 30	4	3	6	3
no opinion	30–64	4	5	8	6
	Over 65	11	12	16	9
Total	Under 30	101	100	101	100
	30-64	100	100	100	101
	Over 65	99	101	100	101

tion on values over which they feel conflict, or when they are not presented with discriminations among which they can reasonably choose. What are the possible explanations for the high "stop crime" proportions among the elderly? Doubtless the fear of crime is a factor. Many elderly are vulnerable and powerless in the face of crime. If one is concerned about crime, even if one has never been a victim personally, the issue becomes the feeling of powerlessness and the anxiety that a person might become a victim or that an accused lawbreaker might seek retribution even while his or her rights are being protected. Often the elderly cannot relocate; they do not have the resources to secure protection from private police and the picture is not one that contains many options.

Yet a substantial proportion of the elderly were noncommittal. While large numbers were willing to curtail rights to control crime, a large number also

Table 9.6
Public Attitude towards Protecting the Rights of the Accused

	Age	1970	1972	1974	1976	1978
All Respondents						
Protect rights of accused (1–3)		29	30	33	28	23
Neutral (4)		15	16	16	14	16
Stop crime (5–7)		42	40	34	40	46
Don't know; no opinion		13	14	17	18	15
Total		99	100	100	100	100
By age						
Protect rights of accused (1–3)	Under 30	39	40	45	37	33
	30–64	30	31	30	27	20
	Over 65	16	14	19	18	18
Neutral (4)	Under 30	17	17	14	14	18
	30–64	15	17	17	16	16
	Over 65	13	11	15	9	10
Stop crime (5–7)	Under 30	34	33	22	36	39
	30–64	43	40	39	41	48
	Over 65	48	50	41	44	51
Don't know; no opinion	Under 30	10	9	19	13	11
	30–64	12	9	14	15	16
	Over 65	23	17	24	30	23
Total	Under 30	100	99	100	100	101
	30–64	100	97	100	99	100
	Over 65	100	92	99	101	102

had no opinion. It is this balance between "no opinion" and "don't know" and the "stop crime" responses that present the fullest, truest picture of the elderly's responses. Understandably, the elderly, more than younger age groups, are fearful of crime. Yet because this fear may be a relatively new feeling, they may still harbor concerns for the rights of the accused developed during their younger years. So their responses range between wanting to stop crime regardless of the rights of the accused and feeling ambivalent about the issue.

THE WAVERING OF TRADITIONAL VALUES

Work, family life, and religion are thought by many to encompass some of America's most traditional values (Tropman 1987, 280–282). Yet they are widely commented upon today as being subject to great strain. Our data shows that values surrounding work and religion are not in any imminent danger. Family orientation does seem to be undergoing some redefinition, even while an overall faith in this institution remains strong (Clark and Martine 1979) (see Tables 9.7, 9.8, and 9.9).

Not nearly as many measures of these values were available as we would have liked, but those we found can provide some general hypotheses of what is happening to these traditional values within the culture. Reported church attendance was used to assess religious orientation, preferences concerning reduction of the hours in the work week to assess work orientation, and attitudes toward the ideal number of children in the family to assess family orientation.

Both change and stability characterized the respondents' attitudes. Change is evident in the slight drop of support for a full forty-hour work week from support levels of the past, the lower proportions that reported regular church attendance, and the preference for a smaller "ideal number of children." These changes, with the exception of the sharply reduced ideal family size, are not dramatic ones, however. Rather, they represent the wavering of traditional

Table 9.7
Public Attitude towards the Issue of Reducing the Hours in a Work Week

	Age	1953	1959	1962	1965
All Respondents					
Should		21	26	31	28
Should not		73	67	61	65
No opinion		6	7	8	7
Total		100	100	100	100
By age					
Should	Under 30	23	22	33	29
	30–64	20	28	32	30
	Over 65	23	22	21	20
Should not	Under 30	73	74	62	68
	30–64	74	65	60	63
	Over 65	71	67	66	69
No opinion	Under 30	4	4	5	4
	30–64	6	7	8	7
	Over 65	7	12	13	11
Total	Under 30	100	100	100	101
	30–64	100	100	100	100
	Over 65	101	101	100	100

Table 9.8
Public Attitude about the Ideal Number of Children in a Family (Percentages)

	Age	1941	1953	1963	1968	1971	1974	1978
All Respondents								
As many as you like, up to family[a]		2	2	7	1	5	0	6
Five or more		12	12	13	9	4	5	4
Four		26	28	35	32	19	13	13
Three		30	28	26	32	29	23	24
Two		27	27	18	25	41	48	51
None to one		2	1	1	1	1	2	2
Total		99	98	100	100	91	91	100
By Age								
As many as you like,	Under 30	2	1	7	—	3	—	—
up to family[a]	30–64	2	3	7	2	6	—	—
	Over 65	6	4	7	1	5	—	—
Five or more	Under 30	7	9	10	6	2	3	—
	30–64	12	12	13	9	5	6	—
	Over 65	21	18	21	13	7	9	—
Four	Under 30	18	24	32	30	13	9	—
	30–64	27	28	35	32	20	15	—
	Over 65	36	34	41	35	22	20	—
Three	Under 30	31	29	28	33	28	25	—
	30–64	32	29	26	33	29	25	—
	Over 65	18	24	24	30	32	28	—
Two	Under 30	40	36	23	31	51	57	—
	30–64	25	26	19	24	39	52	—
	Over 65	17	19	6	18	33	41	—
None to one	Under 30	3	2	0	0	2	3	—
	30–64	2	2	0	1	1	2	—
	Over 65	3	2	0	0	0	2	—
Total	Under 30	101	101	100	100	99	97	—
	30–64	100	100	100	101	100	100	—
	Over 65	101	101	99	97	99	100	—

Note: Exact coding categories are unclear for this question in reputed documents because of the long number of years involved. Interested scholars should check with the Roper Center or the Gallup Organization. Dates sometimes vary between questionnaire administration and reporting.

[a]Asked in 1971, 1974; other, undesignated, in 1978.

Table 9.9
Frequency of Church Attendance (Percentages)

	Age	1952	1956	1958	1960	1962	1964	1966	1968	1970	1972	1974	1976	1978
All Respondents														
Regularly		38	42	42	40	44	42	40	37	37	37	37	37	39
Often		18	18	18	16	16	16	18	15	15	12	12	14	13
Seldom		35	33	32	30	31	30	31	35	29	32	30	28	33
Never; inapplicable		8	6	8	12	9	12	11	13	18	20	21	21	16
Total		99	99	100	98	100	100	100	100	99	101	100	100	101
By age														
Regularly	Under 30	35	43	36	43	38	31	34	32	29	27	25	27	29
	30–64	39	43	45	45	44	43	40	39	38	41	40	39	41
	Over 65	37	41	37	37	51	51	44	39	45	43	46	45	48
Often	Under 30	18	20	17	19	16	18	17	16	20	14	11	16	16
	30–64	18	18	18	18	17	17	19	15	15	11	12	13	12
	Over 65	18	18	20	12	14	14	15	14	12	10	13	13	11
Seldom	Under 30	40	33	40	32	38	37	40	41	30	37	36	31	39
	30–64	35	34	30	32	31	29	31	35	31	31	31	29	31
	Over 65	32	29	32	37	24	24	23	29	22	26	21	23	27
Inapplic-	Under 30	7	4	8	7	7	14	10	11	22	23	28	25	17
able	30–64	8	5	7	5	8	12	10	11	16	17	17	19	16
Never	Over 65	14	13	12	13	12	11	18	19	20	21	21	19	14
Total	Under 30	100	100	101	101	99	100	101	100	101	101	100	99	101
	30–64	100	100	100	100	100	101	100	100	100	100	100	100	100
	Over 65	101	101	101	99	101	100	100	101	99	100	101	100	100

Note: This question has varied somewhat over the years. In 1952, 1956, 1958, 1960, 1962, 1964, 1966, and 1968, it was "Would you say you go to church regularly, often, seldom or never?" In 1970, it was "Would you say you go to church—every week, several times a month, a few times a year, or never?" In 1972, 1974, 1976, and 1978, it was "Would you say you go to (church/synagogue) every week, almost every week, several times a month, a few times a year, or never?"

values, changes occurring within an overall framework of constancy. Even in views on the ideal family size, where the greatest change was evident, one sees only an adjustment from preferring several children to a preference for two children. Among those who view one or no children as ideal (for which about 2% has opted), there has been almost no observable change in forty years. Further, the growing preference for small families may reflect economic conditions as much as family values.

It is in looking at the age breakdowns that a second conclusion emerges. The younger groups are much more likely to be less traditional than the elders. In the 1960s, a slightly higher percentage of younger people preferred a shorter work week, though in general there has been a consistent preference among all ages to retain a forty-hour work week. On the family size question, the elders' ideal of larger families was retained over the years even though the proportion of people holding this ideal diminished for all age groups. In church attendance, the elderly actually reported an increase in regular church attendance, while the younger groups reported a drop. Here, responses of the two age groups do, in fact, go in opposite directions.

In these terms, youth appear to be less "other" oriented than the elders. They are less connected to church, to work, and to children than their older compeers. Contrary to theories which suggest that people become more self-centered as they grow older, these data suggest the reverse: that people in youth are more self-centered and become more other oriented as the process of aging progresses. This pattern is, with a couple of exceptions, present in all the years covered by the surveys. Ideal family size represents such a pattern among the elderly, even though every age group today has more of a preference for smaller families than they did in 1941. The middle-aged group was intermediate on most questions, suggesting a life cycle progression from a greater emphasis upon self and self-reliance to a focus on interdependence and recognizing the importance of collective, interactive postures. This tendency is not overwhelming, by any means, but it is unmistakably present.

WHAT ALL THIS MEANS IN TERMS
OF HATING THE POOR

Pulling the findings together, we can see that the older adults and the younger adults did not differ that much in their attitudes represented here. They both trust the government less.

Some conclusions can be suggested. There appeared to be a trend toward the more "traditional" values of privatism and individual contest (struggle), and a declining support for governmental involvement in a range of policy areas (eclipse of public function). The proportions shift consistently in this direction over a period of time. The concept of, and confidence in, government efficacy, spawned by the twin victories over the Depression and in World War II, may have drawn to a close with the twin defeats of the Poverty Program and Vietnam. In this orientation, the elderly share fully. What is paradoxical here is that the older respondent is in an important way "biting the hand that feeds him or her." Seniors have gained through public function and government, whatever its other flaws. Their experiences—Medicare, the Older Americans Act, the Age Discrimination Act—have all worked in their favor. And yet the negative view of government is in the ascendancy, even among them.

This paradox is worth some thought. It continues the line developed throughout this book, that values and conditions do not relate well together. At least we are not able to explain much about how people feel from what people are. Even interests seemed washed away in the tsunami of dominant values.

What this particular package of findings suggests, then, is that one of the reasons we hate the poor is because we are suspicious of what is required to help the poor when that instrumentality is government. Private charity is fine, but government charity, in a society that was founded by people who fled from government, is to be suspected.

There are, of course, some areas in which they do differ, and emphasis upon larger families is one such area. However, even here they are part of an overall downward trend in family size preference. The public seems to be in more agreement in their views than we might have thought. And if one looks at the data for the 1960s, one does not get a sense of youth alienation either. While it may have been good sense not to trust anyone over thirty, those over thirty were less trusting of the government in the 1960s than younger people (see Table 9.1). Older people, too, were much more likely to think that the government was run by a few big interests than younger people (see Table 9.2). What shows up here is not the radicalism of youth, but, if anything, its idealism.

CONCLUSION

W. F. Ogburn (1928) suggested the concept of "cultural lag." It occurs when an invention forces adjustments in beliefs and values which do not occur immediately (Jaffee 1968, Vol. 11, 279). In cultural lag, values need to catch up to social structure. We would like to introduce the concept of "social lag," in which beliefs and values change but it takes a while for social structure to bring itself into adjustment. Changes in attitudes toward government in a conservative direction occurred long before we actually got such a government. One may then always look for not only a gap among values at any point in time, but a gap between values and social structure. Since both cultural lag and social lag are likely to exist at the same time, there may be a situation of "two-way lag." While such a situation is not neat, it does give policy makers and politicians room for both maneuver and mistake. What does seem likely is that both social lag and cultural lag will compete for policy attention.

NOTE

1. The proportion of "don't knows" has remained fairly steady, as has the proportion of "other, depends" responses. The elderly were slightly more likely, by a percentage point or two, to have no opinion.

Part IV

WHY AMERICA HATES
THE POOR

The attitudes that are revealed here are deep within the American character. They existed during the heyday of social programs—the 1960s and early 1970s—when American society was as concerned about social rights and social wrongs as any time since the Great Depression. Mothers in Detroit, respondents in Kansas City and Boston, and a national sample of welfare directors each revealed suspicion of the poor and programs that serve the poor. Perhaps more ominously, this suspicion was held even among the disadvantaged respondents themselves.

The power of these images, robust during "liberal" times, has increased in the 1990s. They were never too far from the surface. Hate of the poor, like anti-Semitism in Europe, seems to be a deep undercurrent.

The poor—the underclass or status poor and the life cycle poor—are hated because they are threatening. I have made some preliminary suggestions, but in this section I would like to offer some more detailed considerations. Let me share some thoughts from *The Catholic Ethic in American Society*:

American society has always reached out to help others. Communal barn raising and mutual assistance in rural communities have become legendary. Town neighbors have always been ready to lend "a cup of sugar" if you were a bit low. The tendency for neighbor to help neighbor in the daily tasks of living is a historical part of the American experience.

We also help those in serious need. Generous foreign aid is one case in point. And though the United States moved into the welfare state era (providing the use of state power and state resources to those in need) later than other developed countries, for all practical purposes, it is now a welfare state in that it makes substantial public expenditures at federal and state levels for programs like social security, unemployment compensation, and child welfare.

Much help is also provided through private charity. Billions are given in voluntary contributions for those in need—an average of $649 for each of our 93.5 million households in 1991 (Hodgkinson and Weitzman 1992, 1). Nor do gifts of money tell the whole story. Millions of Americans devote untold hours in volunteer work—20.5 billion hours in 1991 (Hodgkinson and Weitzman 1992, 1). For example, in a program called Choice, "recent college graduates work . . . 70-hour weeks for a year for a pittance." They are assigned a small number of juvenile delinquents, the "cream of the crap," and seek to help them (Klein 1994b, 28).

Self-Help

But there is another, careful side to our society's generosity. "Help" often is first thought of as "self-help." Americans have the urge to assist, but they have a hesitancy about assistance as well. Part of the American character celebrates "Yankee ingenuity," doing it yourself and being self-reliant. You can dip into the community pot too often, it seems. As Vidich and Bensman point out in *Small Town in Mass Society* (1968), when neighbors provided that cup of sugar, *they remembered it and had an expectation that the borrower would repay it.* The help was not a gift but a loan.

Moreover, as open as the United States is overall, in smaller groups, its citizens have favored exclusion rather than inclusion of "others." The recent development of the PLUs (*people like us*) group is not new but rather represents an extension of the historical American approaches of isolationism and nativism. "People like us" depicts those who select residences in tight enclave communities, usually with a guard at the community entrance. Communities ("plantations") on Hilton Head Island, South Carolina, for example, have been this way for many years. The guards are a formal and public expression of a deeper set of policies, practices, and values designed to keep people of similar social and ethnic status within an enclave.

Sometimes the enclave concept gets pushed right into the home. Faith Popcorn (1991) talks about modern *cocooning*, a withdrawal into one's own house with everything one needs to do organized around that dwelling: one shops by phone, has food delivered, goes to the movies by watching videos, and so on. Cocooning is "the impulse to get *inside* when everything *outside* gets too scary" (p. 27).

This withdrawal into family or self can be associated with a desire for personal ownership, often quite independent of "need." Attitudes abound that express the sense of "It's mine! You can't have it, even if I don't need it or can't use it." Everyone has "my" snowblower, "my" lawn mower, and "my" car (or, more likely, cars).

This focus on ourselves and what is ours leads to a diminished focus on others and on assisting them in meeting their needs. In today's world, we see many examples of social concern for those in need, but we also see examples of self-absorption, of a narcissism that seems to define the current population as a "me" generation as opposed to an "us" generation.

Suspicion of the Poor

Ambivalence about helping often shifts to suspicion when those Americans called the "poor," the "underclass," the "needy," and the "homeless" are discussed. On the one hand, Americans want to help out. On the other hand, they ask whether the needy person is worthy of help. Adding to their concern is their uncertainty about the process of helping itself. Too much help, they often feel, may sap the recipient's independence and ability to do things for herself or himself.

This concern is often heavily involved with moral disparagement of the poor. People in need are frequently referred to as "them," a fact Joyce Carol Oates acknowledged when she called her novel about the Detroit poor *Them* (1969). "Them," of course, implies an "us," and it is only a half a step or less from "them" and "us" to "we're okay" and "they're not okay" (compare Katz's study of "the undeserving poor," 1989).

When we do help out, we often do so with skepticism and concern about why the recipients are so needy and what they might do with the resources provided. We continue to suspect what Rauschenbusch thought in 1911: "To accept charity is at first one of the most bitter experiences of the self-respecting workingman. Some abandon families, go insane, or commit suicide rather than surrender the virginity of their independence. But when they have once learned to depend on gifts, the parasitic habit of mind grows upon them, and it becomes hard to wake them back to self-support" (p. 238).

We have a sense that the needy will "rip us off." Here is a common example of the attitudes in the daily press and elsewhere. A 1992 column in the *Detroit News* was headlined: "City Merchants' Anti-Panhandling Campaign Raises an Issue of Morality." In that column, Kate DeSmet wrote:

> The Central Business District Association recently handed out 1,200 flyers in Detroit asking people to stop giving money to panhandlers. "Avoid supporting what in most cases is an alcoholic and destructive lifestyle," the posters say. "You need not feel guilty when saying no." Many business owners applauded, but others question the morality of such a move. In a conversation overheard among several Metro Detroit businessmen, one said, "You know, it's never bothered me to give money to someone who walks up to me on the street. If it's because he wants to go and get drunk, I figure that's his problem, but if the guy is hungry and I don't give him anything, then that's what bothers me" [p. 3B].

In Berkeley, California, merchants tried a different tack. They gave out chits you could carry around in your pocket. If you felt like giving to a street person, you could give a chit, redeemable only for food and essential items. This approach seemed to solve a problem for those who wanted to be helpful but were doubtful about the uses to which cash might be put.

For people in the helping professions, experiencing hostile attitudes toward the disadvantaged are a common part of everyday work life. Indeed, many helping professions practitioners feel that the problematic status of those they help somehow rubs off on them. It may be overstating the case to say that Americans *dislike* the poor—but not by a great deal.

Linda Gordon has observed that racism and sexism have played a part in making welfare a "dirty word." And she is surely correct. However, she also says that "no one likes welfare," and she points out that "the poorer and more maligned welfare recipients are, the more difficult it is for them to build political support for improving welfare" (1994, p. B1). Her observations imply that Americans do not like the poor *whoever* they are. Indeed, dislike of the poor antedates what we call welfare today (Aid to Families with Dependent Children, a program of the Social Security Act). While the American people do not withhold basic material support for those in need, we do withhold approval, sympathy, empathy, and understanding. (Tropman 1995, 1–5)

This lack of approval, sympathy, empathy, and understanding is part of what I call hate.

But why should this be so? I think there are basically two reasons. One is that the poor embody our worst thoughts, fears, questions, and feelings of guilt. Hate is a form, then, of "thought management," when the thoughts are, by and large, intolerable, the fears unmanageable, the questions unanswerable, and the quilt unassuageable.

The second reason aggravates the first. In spite of our concerns and worries about social justice, why we have so much when others have so little, we are still driven for more. The worse truth is that we need the resources of the poor and the old. Hate is a precursor to, and justification for, social exploitation. Chapter 10 explores the first problem; Chapter 11 considers the second.

Chapter 10

The Poorfare State: Embodiment and Revelation

WHAT THE POOR MEAN TO THE NONPOOR

What is it, then, that "bugs us" about the poor. Out worst fears are indicated by "fear of falling," as Barbara Ehrenreich (1989) titled her book. In an open society, what goes up may also come down; that is what openness means. You have "choice," but you also have some responsibility for that choice and for the effects of that choice. The fear behind the fear is fear of the lack of control. Openness is, on the one hand, great; on the other hand, it is terrifying. Lack of control also is evident in fear of aging. Aging is another kind of falling, ultimately into death, but before that into uselessness, lack of respect, illness, and geezerhood.

WHAT ABOUT BOB?

It is not only the condition of the poor that causes problems, however; it is the presence of the poor. "Out of sight, out of mind" may work, and has been tried. Ghettoization and physical removal of the poor is a good first step. Then social distance adds to the problem. But the poor always seem to be with us; a sort of nightmare, always turning up, always demanding much and offering little. In the movie *What About Bob?* a psychiatrist has the bad dream turn into reality. Bob, the intrusive client, seems to be omnipresent. One actually becomes uncomfortable with the alleged comedy. It is only funny for a little while. The same problem occurred in the film *Cable Guy*. The fact that two recent films deal with the topic of a repeated noxious presence—and they are billed as comedies—is instructive. They are dark comedies at best, and the latter rings hollow.

The poor embody our society's "Bob" or "Cable Guy." We cannot seem to get rid of them or their demands. It is true that the poor we are always with us. But so what? Why is it an issue at all? The presence of the poor is, itself, a demand. Millions of Americans think the elderly do not get enough respect and are disengaged and alienated from their families when none of that is true. Their presence activates our projections. We cannot just reject them. It is safer to hate them. Societies—and people too, for that matter—have many ways of dealing with the fearsome, the terrible, and the awful. One of these ways is hate. Hate turns the problem around, projects the difficulties onto the victim, and at the same time protects the hater.

THE PROBLEM OF PROVIDING HELP

One approaches the poor with the same caution as one approaches a drowning person in the sea; we want to help, but do not want to get killed in the process. The problem of help—how much and what kind to provide—is an ongoing problem. Some counsel "love," others counsel "tough love." Some say "provide the hungry a fish," others say "teach the hungry how to fish."

On the one hand, there is the concept of simple Christian charity (or one might say Jewish charity or any other kind of religious charity), which provides a historical focus for an organization for help and assistance to those in need. In contradistinction to that orientation is one that might be called "catch the cheaters," in which the dominant orientation is one of suspicion of those who are for the disadvantaged or who use public social services. This perspective conveys a profound conviction that individuals who are poor and needy and are using the services available to them are somehow ripping off the system, and that these individuals are not really "truly" needy.

The elderly, too, are viewed as problematic. Old and young alike separate themselves from the old. Both groups see more problems in the condition of aging than the elderly actually report. Medicare and Social Security are now continually in the papers as problems to be addressed if not solved. What was begun as an entitlement is now perceived as a millstone.

Historical nomenclature—the "deserving poor," the "worthy poor"—present during the boom times of the 1960s and 1970s are now experiencing a vigorous resurgence. Semi-humorous juxtapositions between the truly needy and the worried well are used to embarrass those providing mental health services across the social status spectrum.

CAUSE AND CONDITION

The axis of cultural cloth in American society seems to hang on a dimension of cause versus condition. The powerful theme in American thought seems to emphasize and highlight the cause of poverty, particularly when it can be considered to be the fault of the individual. While getting old per se is certainly not one's "fault," growing old "poorly" can be construed as your fault. Being poor, however, may well be in the view of many respondents their fault or, for those in poverty, my fault. If the causes of your condition are thought to be within your control and you did not take appropriate action to forestall the result, then Americans appear quite unsympathetic to providing assistance.

A subdominant theme, however, stresses the condition. While cause does not go away, it drops lower in thought. Conditions of need which require help should get help. Whether one's actions were or were not the cause of the condition appears to become a secondary consideration.

One way to think about this tension is how parents might answer the phone when their teenager calls and says, "Mom, Dad, there has been an accident with the car!" What is the first thing that comes to the parents' minds as a response? One response could be, "Whose fault was it? Was anyone hurt?" A second response could be, "Was anyone hurt? Whose fault was it?"

In this little example cause and condition, and their various orders of precedence, become crystal clear. American society, I argue, opts for the first response. We are not insensitive to condition, especially when effort is involved. We applaud the blind selling brooms, troubled youth selling candy (even if we do not want candy), and the products of sheltered workshops and junior achievement.

As a fault-oriented society, we tend to select, where possible, variables over which people have control as explainers of conditions, both good ones and bad. In thinking about the lowest class and the next-to-the-lowest class, cause seems to be an important distinguishing feature. Respondents did not pick conditions such as race or gender as explainers of lowest-class status; rather, they picked ones over which it might appear people had more control, such as education and having a job. Similarly, an important feature of the way people think about the old is that the negatives overwhelm the positives, even though those situations of negativism do not seem to actually exist.

Thinking Scary Thoughts

Why do we do this? Why are cause and fault so prominent in our thinking? If you know what caused something to occur (poverty) then you know what to avoid. It is the magical connection of magic, science, and religion. Follow the procedures, do not step on the crack, and then you won't break your grandmother's back. Fault leads to resentment; resentment leads to hate. Hate soothes us, and neutralizes the scary thoughts.

CONCLUSION

The poor are a big problem in American society—a sociological problem. Social welfare experts, social workers, and many run-of-the-mill Americans think the problem of the poor is that they are poor or old. So we have to understand what the poor mean. We need "interpretive explanation." Let us look again at Clifford Geertz (1980): "Interpretative explanation . . . trains its attention on what . . . [the poor] *mean* to those whose institutions, actions, customs, and so on, they are" (p. 167, italics added).

What the poor embody and reveal to us is our fear of downward mobility or aging. By showing up and by being around they force us to deal with that very unpleasantness. Part of it we deal with through helping them (but we resent it); part of it is dealing with ourselves, and that is handled by hate. However, hate justifies something even more. It is a prerequisite for social exploitation. We have more than fear to worry about.

Chapter 11

Social Exploitation

Hate not only soothes and protects us from internal demons; it allows us, through omission and commission, to act out on the hated. We do not feel bound by the same strictures of behavior we would feel if people were, after all, "like us." In the case of the poor, they provide a needed source of resources. It is important for us, the takers, to feel okay about this, especially as we ourselves are less willing to make the kind of efforts we expect of them. Amazing as it may seem, we need the resources of the poor and the elderly. In the period of the surveys here, resources were less of a problem because the economy was growing enormously. Thus, we could fund "social justice" because the costs only meant our own resources grew a bit more slowly. The negativism was thus held at bay. However, the worm turned, the chicken came home to roost, and we had to pay the piper. Poor hate roared out of the cultural closet.

THE GAP BETWEEN NEEDS AND RESOURCES

People in all societies have needs and wants. These needs and wants will exceed available resources at any point in time—in both an absolute and a relative sense—and the gap between them will be maintained. This gap exists in an absolute sense because it is present in every society, developed or underdeveloped, large or small. It is also present in subunits within the society: formal organizations, governments, families, or individuals. One way or another, we all fight the battle of the budget, an attempt to match available resources to needs and wants.

The gap exists in a relative sense because of the concept of "relative deprivation." It is not the amount of actual deprivation an individual has to endure that causes resentment, but rather the amount of deprivation relative to those in a similar position. Hence, in a wealthy society those who are not quite as wealthy may feel relatively deprived compared to those who are wealthy, even though their status may greatly exceed that of the wealthy in another society. To look at it from the other end of the spectrum, it is often pointed out that the poor in Western industrialized countries are better off than the poor in lesser developed countries. This observation seems to mainly comfort academics, since the poor in well-to-do societies feel poor (Himmelfarb 1984).

The gap would not necessarily have to be there, however. Societies could divide their pie equally (Rawls 1985). Or they could use some version of a "from each according to his abilities to each according to his needs" approach. Or they could adjust their consumption to be in line with their resources (or, through thrift, they could even have consumption below their resources).

The problem is that most of us are not frugal, and most societies do not have an ascetic, thrifty culture. Typically, those in power want, and get, more; others are needy. Consider the social system of the wolf as an example: "After the wolf pack has made a kill and the top wolves have full bellies, the other wolves down on the social ladder can eat. If there isn't enough food to go around, only the top wolves eat, and the wolves on the lower end of the totem pole go hungry" (Karnes 1996, 29).

SOCIAL EXPLOITATION, SOCIAL SURPLUS, AND SOCIAL AMELIORATION

In society, as we struggle to make ends meet, to achieve some harmony between needs and wants and resources, we need to find extra resources; usually those which belong to or should belong to others to fill the gap. Direct theft is one possible approach. Another is social exploitation.

Social exploitation is the attempt to secure labor for free or cheap. It is an attempt to force, induce, or convince individuals to contribute their work effort to society at no or low cost. Such a contribution would have an important effect on increasing available social resources.

Social surplus identifies those resources which result from social exploitation. Social surplus is frequently sequestered in organizations, individuals, and families throughout the society and is not available for general use.

Social amelioration refers to those programs and services which stem (in part) from the needs generated by social exploitation. The kinds of ameliorative programs needed will vary from society to society, of course. But exploitation carries with it costs, and societies often seek to provide services which ameliorate or at least tamp down the exploitative costs.

Social Exploitation

Given the gap between needs and wants and resources, societies, as well as organizations, families, and individuals, are faced with the constantly pressing need to increase resources. One way to increase resources is to secure labor contributions inexpensively. If work effort can be secured at below-market rates, then the production needs of society will come closer to the consumption needs. Social exploitation refers specifically to the attempts on the part of society to capture these labor contributions. Important as it is, social exploitation is not the only form of exploitation societies use to secure resources. Environmental exploitation, involving not only animals but also land, plants, and water, is another time-honored location for and form of exploitative behavior. The overharvesting of certain species and the maltreatment of domestic animals are two examples familiar to us all. They represent cheap sources of supply for either sales (furs, buffalo skins, etc.) or labor (horses, oxen, etc.). The ravishment of public land without reclamation and the dumping of materials into rivers and streams are also exploitative in that they allow perpetrators to pay less than the full cost of their product (some organizations in the United States are beginning to assess an added "green tax" to cover environmental costs of their products).

Social exploitation refers particularly to the use of people and an attempt, through human labor, for exploitative perpetrators to reduce the cost of the need and want fulfilling services which they are providing.

Methods of Social Exploitation

There are three major methodologies through which socially exploitative activities are carried out in societies: force, inducement, and conviction (or belief). In the case of force, an individual is coerced into giving his or her services. It is often called slavery. In the case of inducement, there is an exchange in return for services or products, but it is an unfair exchange. The market value test cannot be met, and the victim is, in effect, "ripped off." In the case of conviction, an individual is convinced to give his or her services free of charge.

Social Coercion (Force)

Social coercion is perhaps the most familiar form of social exploitation. Known as slavery, it has a long record in human societies and in this context is a historically important mechanism for securing free labor from subjugated victims by dominant perpetrators. Slaves can be of different races or color, from villages or societies defeated in war, or from other sources. They provide free or very inexpensive labor—one of the most important pressures generating an institution like slavery (however, under certain conditions, paying wages might well be cheaper than keeping slaves).

Another example of social coercion is child labor: the abusive employment of younger workers. Child labor laws in developed countries have been set up precisely to prevent or at least temper this kind of activity. The use of conscription or "draft" mechanisms to secure young men and women for military service is a third example of social coercion.

Social Exchange (Inducement)

In a social exchange, individuals are not forced to give their services for free, but they are not getting fair market value either. Wage discrimination by sex, race, or religion is a classic example of exploitation through social exchange. Individuals are paid less than current market rates for the work they are doing, thus lowering the cost of the product or service to the exploitative perpetrator. The social ramifications of this behavior should not be overlooked. The structure motivation for "workaholism" certainly does not spring totally from within the individual but represents a socially structured set of inducements. Workaholism, a general term used here to indicate contributions to an organization over and above that for which the individual is being compensated, represents a tremendous source of organizational wealth. It is no accident that organizations are always looking for highly motivated workers (Schaef and Fassel 1988).

A second form of socially exploitative exchange might be called "guilty contributions." Here, employees are made to feel they should overinvest in their workplace. This mechanism is often used in social agencies, and is an important vehicle for cost tamping.[1]

The rip-off is another form of social exploitation which usually occurs on the consumer side. A producer manages to exchange a product of small value for cash well in excess of the product's worth. The numerous roofing and siding salesmen who dot the urban landscape selling inferior products at superior prices represent a well-known case of this phenomenon. On a more global scale, there is the colonial impulse, in which entire countries serve as customers for the exports of a dominant society.

Social Co-optation (Conviction or Belief)

Social co-optation is a method of social exploitation in which individuals give their services, inexpensively or for free, rather than being forced or bargained with. A classic example is "voluntarism." Here, individuals donate their time, energy, and effort to "good" causes. They do not feel exploited, they feel inspirited and uplifted. The socially structured set of norms and values in which such individuals grew up sets the stage for this feeling.[2] Just to give one example of the magnitude involved, one study for the United States in 1983 suggested that $40 billion was an appropriate estimated amount of the worth of voluntary contributions in the nonprofit sector for that year

(Tropman and Tropman 1987). That is truly a staggering sum and one which gives some sense of the amounts involved: It is 200 thousand person years of work.

Job or role diminishment is another socially co-optative mechanism. For example, sexism, ageism, racism, any "ism" which creates a diminished sense of self and self-worth. While such diminishment may not necessarily result in exploitation, it frequently does, and it sets the stage for social coercion or social exchange. For instance, if women are socialized to believe they are not as capable as men, they will not be as likely to demand equal market value for their services, and will be "satisfied" with a lesser return.

Sometimes it is the job which is diminished, thus undermining an individual's ability to secure adequate compensation for it. The garbage man is a classic case in point. Very little could be more important to society than the regular and adequate disposal of its waste products, and yet we have created a set of norms and expectations around this important job that diminish rather than enhance its importance. It is the subtle operation of role and job diminishment processes which fuel demands for "comparable worth."

Another example in the area of work devaluation is discussed by Arlie Hochschild (1983) in her work *The Managed Heart*. She uses her study of stewardess training to show how "emotion work"—an important component of much work done by women—is devalued and denied while at the same time being central to the functioning of the system (in this case, the airplane).

None of these mechanisms work independently. All are needed. When individuals are drafted into the armed services, they are often paid something (inducement added to coercion) and frequently exhorted with sayings that they are "contributing to their country" (a little social co-optation is added). Any form of social exploitation will doubtless rely on some combination of coercion, exchange, and co-optation as a way to sustain the practices in question.

GAP PERSISTENCE

One might ask why the gap between needs and resources persists and why it would be maintained? Wouldn't the gap narrow, especially in the wealthier societies, with increasing productivity and increasing wealth over time? That apparently is not the case. There appear to be several reasons why the gap continues.

The first reason is relative deprivation. In any society, some individuals will have more and some less. Thus, while the needs and wants of some individuals may indeed be satisfied, the needs and wants of others will probably not be. The very fact that some needs and wants are satisfied but not all generates unfavorable social comparison and probably fuels additional sets of demands.[3] An important element here, too, is that in some cases "basic" needs (food, etc.) are not being met for some, while more "advanced" needs are being met for others.

A second reason might be called "the decay of ends." As Merton (1957) has pointed out in his discussion of the means/end chain, there is an interaction between means and ends. Needs and wants represent one kind of ends, and certainly the wants fraction becomes larger as the society becomes wealthier, since basic needs are indeed met. But, as Albert Hirschman (1982) has pointed out in his book *Shifting Involvements*, ends once achieved tend to decay. Disappointment sets in, and new preferences arise. It is for this reason that the gap continues, because the ends are continually being extended.

A third reason is that the very concept of ends itself suggests a singleness, which is not really the case. Most societies, like most persons, have multiple and competing ends which are desired to be achieved. As one set of ends is achieved, leaving aside the issue of disappointment, another set of ends may appear more possible, more desirable, or more appropriate. It is often called the "revolution of rising expectations."

THE LEVEL OF EXPLOITATION

Given the pervasiveness of social exploitation, it is possible to note that some societies' systems and subsystems overall are more exploitative than others. This is because social exploitation can vary depending on the societally achieved balance between norms of sufficiency versus norms of acquisition as fundamental operatives.[4]

Norms of sufficiency tend to dampen the power of relative deprivation and the need to acquire. One can be satisfied when "enough" has been achieved. On the other hand, norms of acquisition tend to support a relatively endless round of activities and achievements. No amount of money is enough; no amount of power, status, or reward is sufficient. The very achieving of a particular goal requires that it be set aside and the next goal established. Competitive sports, especially those with time or distance performance measures, can be seen as an example of acquisitive dominance. If the four-minute mile is run, then 3.99 becomes the next goal. If someone throws a javelin a certain number of record yards, then those yards plus a fraction become the next goal. Against this set of norms, the "personal best" concept is set, a sufficiency concept in which an individual seeks to measure himself or herself against internal standards of performance and accomplishment rather than external ones.

Acquisitive dominance tends to involve insensitivity to human needs in the production process. "Inhumane" training schedules for athletes to achieve marginal increments in national or international times and distances represents an example. But the attempt to continually extend one's power, influence, and wealth is often associated with an insensitivity to the impacts that these extensions are having on others. Furthermore, acquisitive dominance can be enhanced through social exploitation. The society interested in acquisition can acquire more through exploitation than could be acquired without it. Hence, there tends to be an affinity between exploitation on the one hand and acquisitive dominance on the other.

POOR HATE AND SOCIAL EXPLOITATION

America has had it own history of socially exploitative patterns: slavery and the exploitation of people of color, child labor, exploitation of immigrants, and the diminishment of the role of women. For many years we conscripted individuals into the army through a draft system and used mental patients and prisoners as workers. This list omits animal exploitation, which generated the founding of the Society for the Prevention of Cruelty to Animals, and environmental exploitation, which has led to the development of numerous environmental rights groups.

Our history also contains an opposition to these exploitative activities, and in the last half of the twentieth century important strides were taken to reduce exploitative activities. The rights revolution of the 1960s, beginning perhaps with Rosie the Riveter in World War II and *Brown v. Board of Education* in 1954, generated a cultural pressure to deal with an important number of exploitative centers within American society. The affluence of the 1960s also made exploitative patterns perhaps clearer and made it easier for individuals to see how rectification might be made. In any event, one can speak of the rights revolution in the sense that a number of rights were reasserted, most of which focused on stopping exploitative activity with respect to particular groups in question. Inroads were made on social exploitation and improvements were generated.

But restoring rights costs money. After all, one of the socially generative reasons for social exploitation in the first place was to secure labor for free or cheap. If one is going to begin to pay individuals to join the army, not use prisoners and patients to do institutional labor, and pay women and Blacks at rates equivalent to their white male counterparts, the cost of doing society's business is going to go up. Not only is free labor lost, but additional income is required. One way, therefore, that one can look at the burgeoning American deficit in the late 1980s is to see it as an example of what a society might do when it does not have the cash to pay its way, and the gap between needs and wants and resources becomes too great: It borrows (and in effect shifts the exploitative burden to future generations).

But the borrowing solution is one that has so many obvious costs that opposition to it is developing on all sides. New solutions are needed, and two general types of solutions are possible. One is to restrain needs and wants. It is unlikely that we will opt for this solution. There are ethos (Quakerism, Puritanism) and recent writings (Schumaker [1973], *Small Is Beautiful*; Elgin [1993], *Voluntary Simplicity*) that advocate restraint and simplicity, but given America's "consuming" history, it is unlikely that we will practice sufficient restraint to reduce needs and wants sufficiently.

The other solution is to find new groups to exploit. The poor seem great targets. To be a successful victim of exploitation, a group must have several features. One is that it must be large enough to have and use resources which can be taken. Second, the group has to be politically weak (children) or vulnerable to guilt so that the exploitation can proceed. Third, the group has to have resources you need. The poor fit all categories.

The Status Poor

From those who have less, more shall be taken. The underclass is an excellent source of exploitative material. It is sizable. Labor is available. It can be intimidated (as we have seen) into thinking that their status is their fault. Hence, they are psychologically vulnerable to accepting poor housing, limited services, episodic work, and so on. We are getting them to work for free or cheap.

Consider the development of the low-paying, off-again–on-again (employment "at will") jobs with no benefits. These jobs are often at places that require transportation (not provided) and child care (not provided), so that the actual sustainable dollars from such work is negligible. It is no wonder many preferred to spend some time on public welfare. There, Medicaid and food stamps helped out. However, opponents of those programs argued we were "creating dependency."

The situation gets worse. Consider the "Clinton" welfare reform bill of 1996 (I put President Clinton in apologetic quotes here because the ideas in this welfare reform bill came from both Democrats and Republicans). For a time, anyway, it will end "welfare as we know it," but it reminds scholars of the poor law reform of 1834 in England, a harsh, conservative document (Garvin and Tropman 1992, 7). Children will be harmed. Support will be truncated. And, delightfully from the point of view of the theory of social exploitation, these cost reductions (and cash recapture) will mean recipients will have to work cheap to retain benefits. Unions are belatedly beginning to realize that the work recipients do may undercut union jobs.

National programs like this one have had state precursors. Many states had already cut General Assistance.[5] The Governor of New Jersey, Christine Todd Whitman, cut taxes, but the civil servants have not had a raise in several years. It sounds like work cheap to me.

The result of welfare reform, then, is that work will be provided free and cheap. This means that money which would have had to be paid for this work is now available for other purposes, probably middle-class purposes. In addition, costs are being cut and money saved. Again, money saved is now available for other purposes.

What might these purposes be? Robert Dole made a 15-percent tax cut the centerpiece of his campaign. That money would have had to come from either saving and thrift, or social exploitation. I would bet on the exploitation. Essentially, the "haves" need a bit more. The economy is not growing as fast as it did in the 1960s, so that presents one problem. And we have counterpressures for pay equity (it is harder to exploit women in the workplace) and so on, so costs are growing.

The Life Cycle Poor

A second good potential target for exploitation is the older American. There are at least five reasons. First, the elder population fraction is increasing. Those over sixty-five are moving from about 11 percent of the population to possibly 20 percent. Currently in Florida, which has the highest percentage of elderly residents, around 17 percent of the population are elderly. The numbers are there.

Second, the older adult population is potentially more vulnerable. Age itself creates some vulnerabilities, and there are more women among the elderly group, which adds a vulnerable element. Overall, the health of the elderly population is not as good as the non-elderly, and the extent that the group is ill adds another vulnerable spot (Estes 1983).

Third, the elderly lack a specific social role or social assignment around which they can organize and through which they could negotiate with the rest of society. Being a grandparent or retired are not socially dynamic roles. Grandparenting is occasional and nonspecific in its assignments, and the role of the elder as sage or patriarch has diminished with increased migration and the rise of the nuclear family; retirement is quite empty with respect to socially useful tasks. Hence, were society to ask (or force or demand) the elderly for socially exploitative contributions, the older adult does not have a socially contributory base around which to organize and from which to demur ("I'm raising kids"; "I'm working").[6]

Fourth, the group has gained heavily from social legislation in the past twenty-five years or so. Not only have the elderly enjoyed improvements in Social Security and the development of a medical care program (Medicare), among other federal initiatives, but there have been numerous state and local initiatives as well. Such local initiatives include senior discounts from local drug stores, plumbers, and service establishments (Lammers 1983).

Last, the older adult, on average, is better off than had been thought. While it is certainly true that there are large archipelagos of poverty, there are also substantial areas where the elderly are well-off. This altered situation (altered at least from the public impression of elderly poverty) has not gone unnoticed (Smolensky, Danziger, and Gottschalk 1988; Fallows 1982).

The elderly may be a tougher target than the status poor. They have more resources with which to fight. They vote, and the American Association of Retired Persons (it has many members who are not retired—membership eligibility begins at fifty) is an active political group.

However, the signs of exploitation are not only on the horizon, they are in the harbor. Society could demand additional tax income, or could delay or change current benefits. Movement in this direction is already underway.

Recent tax legislation added some components of Social Security income to the tax rolls (when combined with other income). Benefits that were previously enjoyed are now less than they were. Similar tax changes have removed the age-related exemption (an exemption for being over sixty-five) that had been available to older taxpayers on federal returns.

There is much discussion in the public press about the cost of medical care, particularly for older adults. Such discussion is ominous, if not specifically prognostic, because it sets the stage for benefit reduction and benefit alteration. Consider the numbers of public pronouncements about volunteer efforts on the part of older adults to help other older adults with health problems. Conference discussions include reports of plans where elders help other elders. All these initiatives, and others too numerous to mention here, may in some narrow sense be correct. It may be important to make certain adjustments in the tax system. It may be important to remove certain exemptions at certain times. It may be important to deal with rising medical costs. The problem, however, occurs when one puts these changes into a pattern and links that pattern to the larger context. It is this larger context of the need for societal victims that makes one wonder, and regardless of the motivation within any policy system for a particular change, the function of such a change may serve entirely different ends. That may in part be the problem the elderly are facing today.

SOCIAL EXPLOITATION AND POOR HATE

To take resources, one must have a reason. If the reason is hard to justify ("I want more, so I will have some of yours"), reasons need to be constructed. Attitudes toward the poor are such a construction. Negative attitudes add psychological solace to the whole picture: If I am going to take from you, it is nice to hate you; then I not only do not feel bad, I can even feel good about it.

CONCLUSION

Social exploitation—the securing of labor resources for free or cheap—seems to be a universal result from the gap between needs and wants (societal, organizational, familial, and individual) and available resources (also societal, organizational, familial, and individual). Many forms of social exploitation have existed over history. Karl Marx (1902), in looking at the relationship between capital and labor, was looking at one particular form of social exploitation as manifest in one particular historical period, but the historical form and choice of predators and victims may and doubtless will change. For Marx, class conflict based on one's position in the division of labor was central.

A future America will see class-related and age-related conflict or generational conflict replacing occupational conflict. The affluent citizens and the younger citizens will most likely unite against the underclass and older. Michael Lind (1995) feels this process is already well underway.

The new American architecture reflects the . . . evolution of American society from Republicanism to feudalism. Downtown office complexes begin to resemble medieval castles—connections of towers, connected by skyways and sealed off from the growing horde of the enemployable poor. . . . [In the future] Dad will bask in the Caribbean sun sketching out marketing designs on his laptop computer, while Mom keeps an eye on baby, via satellite, as she flies from New York to Frankfort to Tokyo. Off camera, never seen, is the Latina who actually changes Baby's diapers. (pp. 35–47)

NOTES

1. Guilty contributions may not be all that is operating here. The individual workaholic may view these "overages" as a risk investment. That is, he or she may be putting in more time in the hope or reaping rewards in the future and, on an individual basis, such an investment could be perfectly understandable. However, on the aggregate basis it still operates as a source of social exploitation and a generative center for organizational wealth. To give a quick example, consider the following: Suppose everyone worked fifty hours a week instead of forty in order to achieve a promotion in a particular firm. Since there is only one promotional space available, the individual who worked fifty-one hours gets the job. However, the organization gets to enjoy (though the employees may not) the results of ten extra hours of contribution from all of its workers.

2. A similar point might be made here with respect to voluntarism that was made with respect to risk investment for upward mobility, and at the individual level it might indeed make sense. A particular individual might well feel the need to share his or her labor with the community in which he or she lives. However, the substantial social benefit from the aggregate of such contributions cannot be overlooked.

3. One place where this can be seen in relatively small compass is in union negotiations, or in fringe benefit negotiations in organizations. It appears there is a maximum to minimum cycle: What was the maximum in one year becomes the minimum for the next year in that same organization. Hence, there is never a point at which one can rest or "take a breather" with respect to other organizations. Any negotiator begins by looking to see what the best package achieved was. That then becomes the goal to strive for.

4. The work-achievement motivation, or need to achieve (see Atkinson 1968, 27–33), may, in this framework, be thought of as "acquisition motivation" or "need-to-acquire."

5. Public Assistance usually came in categories. There was AFDC and SSI (Supplemental Security Income) for the disabled, the blind, and the elderly. These programs were state and federal programs. A poor man with no family could only get general assistance, a state-only program. That is why states could end them.

6. It is important to stress the difference between what any individual older adult may actually do and what society assigns the age grade to be responsible for. It is certainly true that there are a lot of older adults who are in fact working, but society views this as a choice, not a requirement (however true or untrue that may be with respect to the individual case).

Chapter 12

Mirror of Destiny

I have argued that America hates the poor. Perhaps readers will think "hate" is too strong a word. Maybe an "anti-poor" conceptual frame would be better. I could than have anti-poor and hope that it would have the same usage as, say, anti-Semitism. Perhaps the "ism" would work. Then to racism and sexism I could add "poorism." It all amounts to the same thing. Hate seems to say it well.

Hating the poor is a deep cleavage in American society. It is becoming more so as we end the twentieth century. While it has always been present, other targets were also prominent and are still prominent today.

IS IT REALLY RACE?

Race is clearly something that changes America into Americas. Myrdal (1944) pointed out the division between Blacks and whites in *An American Dilemma*. At the time of the riot report from the National Commission on Civil Disorders (Kerner Commission 1968), this was what they had to say: "This is our basic conclusion: Our nation is moving toward two societies, one black, one white—separate and unequal" (p. 1). The problems were in three areas and their intersection and acceleration: poverty, education, and environment (urban ghettoization).

One year later, Urban America (1969) assessed the progress which had been made. Their conclusion was that "The nation has not reversed the movement apart. Blacks and whites remain deeply divided in their perceptions and experiences of American society" (p. 116). The more things change, the more things remain the same.

I think it is important to stress, however, that hating the poor is not racism, though there are surely interconnections. The poor were a problem before the country was born, and no doubt will continue to be a problem for years to come. I think, therefore, it is possible to reject the hypothesis that hate of the poor is really cryptoracism. Clearly racism is a problem. It is, as Myrdal (1944) has argued, "an American dilemma." But all cultural conundrums do not have to be reduced to one. A pluralistic society, America seems to be able to have a plurality of hatreds as well.

DOES AMERICA REALLY HATE THE POOR?

The answer is yes, we do. We do not like to admit it, but for us the poor represent the mirror of our own destiny, the reflection of what, in an open society, we could become. Even the poor—status poor or life cycle poor—distance themselves from themselves. "Those people, those others, them" are disliked across the class structure.

What this observation—the self-distancing—means is that the poor are not only people, they are positions. We do not like many of the people in poverty, or the position of poverty itself.

THE PSYCHOLOGY OF POOR HATE AND ANTI-POORISM

We hate poverty and the poor because poverty brings out our scariest thoughts and provokes our worst fears. As Shakespeare wrote, "The fault dear Brutus, is not in our stars, but in ourselves" (*Julius Caesar*, I.ii., 139–140).

Hating the poor is thus a way to relieve the anxiety within and reassure ourselves. Hate exists as a psychological control mechinism. Rejecting the victim and the position means that one rejects the possibility of oneself being that person or in that position. Hate, too, is active. It falls under the rule of "the best defense is a good offense."

But it is also the case, that for many Americans, it would be deeply troubling to think we hate the poor. I have had long discussions with people who gave example after example of a poor person whom they knew and liked while at the same time talking about tough love for the poor and supporting plans to force everyone to work. Part of hating the poor is hating the position of poverty while at the same time supporting and appreciating specific individuals who are poor. How can this be?

The late Dan Katz, Professor of Psychology at the University of Michigan, explained it as the difference between *in general* thoughts (position-type thoughts) and *in particular* thoughts (person-type thoughts). Think of a restaurant you dislike but, because of some circumstance, you eat there anyway. And you have a great meal. As you are thinking about this situation, Katz would say that in general you do not like this particular restaurant, but in particular you had a good meal there. We can keep our in generals from being influenced by our in particulars up to a point. And, to the point here, negative in generals are more than a little resistant to positive in particulars. That means that not only can we understand the mechanics of why people can use poor hate as a psychological control mechanism while liking and supporting particular individuals, but suggests, as well, one reason that poor hate is so resistant to change.

THE SOCIOLOGY OF POOR HATE AND ANTI-POORISM

Poor hate is also sustained by the cultural system. Our commitment to getting ahead, achievement, opportunity, freedom, and open social structure are all values with a downside. There is the possibility of lack of achievement, the peril of lack of opportunity, the lack of responsibility that freedom brings, and the uncertainty and lack of control that is the heart of an open society. Poor hate is deeply embedded in the values of our country. If this guess is anywhere close to the truth, hating the poor will not go away. We take it with us. Why, then, does America hate the poor? Because of our values. It is the poorfare culture.

Readers may argue that I have not proven my case. I agree. Indeed, it is not clear what would even constitute proof in this case. What I think I have done is to advance a plausible interpretive explanation for an abiding, resiliant pattern in American culture. It is a hypothesis that others will examine and challenge. Bringing up the idea of poor hate and providing a provisional answer to the question, "Does America hate the poor?" will get the discussion going, and it may lead us to some new strategies.

LESSONS FOR THE TWENTY-FIRST CENTURY?

There are several lessons I think we can draw from this analysis and exploration. One lesson is that the past really is prologue. Much of the rhetoric about the poor has been more or less the same since America began, and, before that, in England. If history repeats itself, as it seems to be doing at the end of the century with welfare reform, we can expect much of the same in the future: more liberal, then less liberal, then somewhat more liberal, then somewhat less liberal policies, alternating, more or less, like a sinewave through history.

A second lesson is that the dislike of the poor resides within us as a downside of values we cherish and orientations we support. In spite of many years and many programs—the New Deal, the Fair Deal, the Great Society—it seems that latent within the children of those generations was support for the welfare reform of the late 1990s. And, as the data here show, even within the heyday of the welfare state significant amounts of negatives were still present, waiting—sometimes quietly, sometimes not—for their chance to return to respectability and currency. Perhaps, like a virus, it needs the right "host" context and conditions to become activated.

A third lesson is that, apparently, the springs of culture are tightly wound. Cultural transmission—the passing of feelings, ideas, and values—from one generation to the next is a complex procedure. As any parent knows, the job of teaching "up close and personal" seems like a Sisyphian task. Kids, particularly, seem immune to culture. Some cultural dispositions, like political party identification, for example (see Tropman 1987, Table 4), act so powerfully over time one would think they are "inherited" rather than taught. Antipoorism is apparently like this. It is absorbed, remains present even when the surface culture is going the other way, and then springs back. It apparently can leapfrog generations, and it can do so forcefully.

The fourth lesson is that interventions have to be carefully constructed so that the intervention does not trigger the very conditions and events that will destroy it. If the poor are really a threat to the nonpoor, then sympathy for them has to be carefully marketed, as it were. Packaging matters. For example, the welfare state in Europe was marketed (if the creators of it thought of it as marketing) as a civic necessity. Otto von Bismark argued that Germany could not be great unless workers had some protections. It is much as we market education. We argue that all citizens in a democracy need education, and have built a broad accessible system in every nook and cranny of our country (one that, albeit, needs improvement at the moment). Pushing this parallelism a bit, consider what would happen if welfare and eldercare were rationalized as education is. It would be, and we would have, a different world.

An example will drive this marketing point home. Looking at Europe again, we can see that Europe used soldier rather than mother as the basis for part of their welfare state argument (Skocpol 1992). Society apparently felt it would be easier to gain acceptance for soldiers rather than mothers. England, illustratively, introduced the Beveridge Report on November 20, 1942.[1] England was under attack at the time from Germany. The state, in effect, promised to care for the soldiers and their families if the society survived.

There is another interesting thing about the Beveridge Report. Its actual title is "Social Insurance and Allied Services." The social insurance idea— you chip in, you get to draw out—has been an important piece of spin doctoring for years. I call it "spin doctoring" because almost everyone seems to disagree about what social insurance really is, should be, must be, could be, and so on. Regardless of anyone's answer, this seems to go better when it is called insurance than when it is not.

WHAT CAN WE USE FROM THIS ANALYSIS?

Looked at together, these four lessons provide some guidance for us in policy making and programming. Given that resentments from the past will crop up in the future, two practical directions seem to emerge. One of them is to expect the past to reappear. Social change agents and social policy makers always seem surprised that the attitudes and emotions of poor hate emerge in program pronouncements and proposals long after they were presumed dead. Anti-Semitism has much to teach here. The battle is a constant one. And it should not generate resentment, though we may, of course, feel resentment. Weeding is always something a healthy garden needs.

A second suggestion is to use and learn from the past, in programmatic terms. I am always surprised at how someone comes up with a program—"let us send kids out in the country"—utterly oblivious, apparently, that this has been tried before. It seems trite and obvious to borrow from the past, but what has worked before has not always been continued, and can be used again. What was opposed before will, no doubt, be opposed again. In these days of rapid change, looking to the past is not the most obvious approach, perhaps, but it can help.

Conflicting values become actual conflicts. Let me simply outline a new set of value pairs. I call them controlling American values and moderating American values. Each is a way of approaching a key dimension in our society: How do I conceptualize myself? How do I approach others? What are the rules, the processes, and the goals that are important? How do I think about assigning responsibility? On what basis do I provide help to others? A value system retains its integrity, meaning, purpose, and vitality because it meets the needs of the people who hold it and provides a useable framework for daily life.

But no value system meets all needs or is always applicable. We know this from daily experience. For example, we know there are conditions where one has to draw on one's broader identification with family and kin. We also know there are occasions when one needs to draw on one's own internal sense of being and oneness. It is thus more a question of dominance of one value and subdominance of other values. Pushed too far, any value becomes problematic. Controlling values need moderating ones. Hence, we all have competing values within us. Those of us who are committed to dominant values carry subordinate ones with us. Those of us for whom subdominant values are more prominant carry dominant ones within us. Often the springs of culture cause a "cultural flip," and we see abrupt changes from one to the other. Those who have only one set of values we call zealots.

Table 12.1 shows a new set of value pairs. Controlling American values, as I read them, emphasize individualism (solo self). They are competitive, but stress playing by the rules (fair play). Character is stressed (good or bad char-

Table 12.1
A New Set of Value Pairs

Value Dimension	Dominant Attitude ALPHA	Subdominant Attitude BETA
1. Self	Solo self	Ensemble self
Subordinate values	Team	Separation
2. Others	Competitive	Cooperative
Subordinate values	Mercy/Sufficiency	Individuation
3. Rules	Fair play	Fair share
Subordinate values	Exceptions	Primus Inter Pares
4. Process	Either/or	Up and down
Subordinate Values	Mix & Match	Core Character
5. Goals	Optimizing	Satisficing
Subordinate Values	Better	Best
6. Responsibility	Cause	Condition
Subordinate Values	Predisposing Cause	Predisposing Condition
7. Bases of Help	Worthy	Needy
Subordinate Values	Community Conditions	Effort
8. State Disposition	Poorfare culture	Welfare state

acter). One should strive for the most of anything: grades, scores, money, status. Fault is a common theme of conversation (cause orientation). People are helped if they are "worthy."

The subdominant American values stress other themes. Here the family self, the neighborhood self, and the community self are important parts of identification. Cooperation is important. While rules count, fair share (in kid soccer, everyone must play) is vital. Character is recognized but not seen as immutable; after all, "There but for the grace of God go I." People can and do change. Alcoholics Anonymous proves that. You cannot have much if others have none. Fault is tempered (as in the medical area) and help is provided because of the condition you are in. Help is then need based, not character based.

Poorfare culture is driven by dominant values. The welfare state is sustained by moderating values. The tension between them is a healthy one, as long as the imbalance does not become too severe. But the problem we face is that what should be a balance too often becomes drawn apart into bitter battles, the "poorfares" in one corner and the "welfares" in the other. Each side denies the validity of its own subdominant side.

Hence, what seems like an obvious solution, and in some cases may be an obvious solution—drawing on the subdominant part of each value system—not only does not work but, in the words of one of my students, "exasperates" the problem. Hence, something new is needed. That "something new" is contained in the list of new value pairs. It is the concept of subordinate, rather than subdominant values. A subordinate value moderates the dominant value but leaves it intact. One is not asking to change the balance, but simply to temper the expression. In many cases, that may be enough.

In each case, there is a moderating value within the prominent value, whether that value is a dominant one or a subdominant one for the culture as a whole. In the list, I have placed the subordinate below the prominent one as an additional communicating device. This suggests that the subordinate value resides within the bigger value, rather than being an alternative to it.

Hence, solo self can be moderated by an emphasis on team; competitive orientation can be moderated by emphases on mercy and sufficiency. Fair play—an emphasis on rules—can be modulated by an emphasis on exceptions to the rules. An either/or position is tempered with a stress on mixing and matching. Optimizing can be softened through an emphasis that "better" can sometimes be okay. A narrow "cause" orientation, often precipitating in nature (what came just before the event in question), is modulated by a discussion of predisposing situations. A discussion of whether a person is worthy of help can benefit from some consideration of community conditions. For example, it is hard to find work when the unemployment rate is very high. The same thing is true with those on the "other side." This is a strategy of "immunity" more or less, using the "carriers" own dominant commitments as a source of program building and rationale.

This approach, of course, is where marketing comes in. Emphasizing subordinate rather than subdominant values, may make the task easier. Nonetheless, changes and reversals will occur. That happened in the 1980s and 1990s, when negativism blossomed. The solution is not to hate the hater; we would just be hating ourselves. Rather, the solution is to work toward stronger tempering values. We will not give up American values, and hence the poor will always be problematic. But we can temper our national culture. The tools are there.

CONCLUSION

The poor will always be with us because, in a sense, they are us. What is important is to recognize how profoundly the strengths of our culture create problems for the disadvantaged, and try in a number of ways to create modulation rather than conflict and hate. When the battles get to the right way and the wrong way (and the right way just happens to be my way and the wrong way just happens to be your way), policy flips and flops and grinds to a halt, each victor throwing out what the previous villians had done.

The status poor and the life cycle poor deserve our attention and our respect. Help is not a handout, sympathy need not be without standards, empathy does not have to be empty of expectations. Indeed, a great society should have great expectations.

NOTE

1. This report is widely considered to be a founding document of the welfare state.

References

Achenbaum, W. A. (1983). *Shades of Grey*. Boston: Little, Brown.

Achenbaum, W. A. (1978). *Old age in a new land*. Baltimore: Johns Hopkins University Press.

Ahlstrom, S. E. (1972). *A religious history of the American people*. New Haven: Yale University Press.

"Ann Landers." (1978). *Detroit Free Press*, 11 February, 133.

Atkinson, J. (1968). Achievement motivation. In *International Encyclopedia of the Social Sciences*, ed. D. Sills. Vol. 1. New York: The Free Press.

Bell, D. (1976). *The cultural contradictions of capitalism*. New York: Basic Books.

Benjamin, A. E., Jr. (1977). Welfare variations among counties: An analysis of policy choice. Ph.D. diss., University of Michigan.

Blau, P. M., and O. D. Duncan. (1967). *The American occupational structure*. New York: Wiley.

Butler, R. (1975). *Why survive: Being old in America*. New York: Harper & Row.

Cameron, C. (1975). *Attitudes of the poor and attitudes toward the poor: An annotated bibliography*. Madison: Institute for Research on Poverty, University of Wisconsin.

Clark, R., and G. Martine. (1979). Americans still in a family way. *Public Opinion* 2 (5): 16–19.

Cloward, R. A., and I. Epstein. (1967). Private social agencies disengagement from the poor. In *Community action against poverty*, ed. G. Brager and F. Purcell. New Haven: Yale University Press.

Coleman, R. P. (1973). Personal communication with author, 15 June.

Coleman, R. P., and B. L. Neugarten. (1971). *Social status in the city*. San Francisco: Jossey Bass.

Cumming, E. (1967). *Allocation of care to the mentally ill, American style*. In *Organizing for community welfare*, ed. Mayer Zald. Chicago: Quadrangle Books.

Darnay, A. J., ed. (1994). *Statistical record of older Americans*. Detroit: Gale Research.

·Dear, R. B. (1989). What's right with welfare? The other face of AFDC. *Journal of Sociology and Social Welfare* 16 (2): 5–43.

DeSchwenitz, K. (1943). *England's road to social security from the statute of laborers in 1349 to the beverage report of 1942*. Philadelphia: University of Pennsylvania Press.

Desmet, K. (1992). City merchants' anti-panhandling campaign raises an issue of morality. *Detroit News*, 10 July, 1.

Duncan, O. D. (1968). *Socioeconomic background and occupational achievement; extensions of a basic mode*. Washington, D.C.: U.S. Department of Health, Education, and Welfare, Office of Education, Bureau of Research.

Ehrenreich, B. (1989). *Fear of falling*. New York: Harper & Row.

Elgin, D. (1993). *Voluntary simplicity: Toward a way of life that is outwardly simple, inwardly rich*. Rev. ed. New York: Morrow.

Estes, C. (1979). *The aging enterprise*. San Francisco: Jossey Bass.

Fallows, J. (1982). Entitlements. *Atlantic Monthly*, November, 51–59.

Feagin, J. R. (1972). *Subsidizing the poor: A Boston housing experiment*. Lexington, Mass.: Lexington Books.

Fischer, D. H. (1978). *Growing old in America*. New York: Oxford University Press.

Garvin, C., and J. E. Tropman. (1992). *Social work: An introduction*. Englewood Cliffs, N.J.: Prentice Hall.

Geertz, C. (1980). Blurred genres: The refiguration of social thought. *The American Scholar* 49 (2): 165–179.

Gilligan, C. (1982). *In a different voice: Psychological theory and women's development*. Cambridge: Harvard University Press.

Gockle, B. (1966). *Silk stockings and blue collars*. Report #114. Chicago: National Opinion Research Center.

Gordon, L. (1994). How "welfare" became a dirty word. *The Chronicle of Higher Education* 40: B1–B2.

Greer, G. G. (1978). What's happening to the American family: How it sounds to us. *Better Homes and Gardens* 56 (9): 81–82, 86, 88, 90, 92.

Greer, G. G., and K. Keating. (1978). What's happening to the American family: A report from more than 300,000 readers. *Better Homes and Gardens* 56 (6): 23–24, 26, 28, 30, 33, 34, 36.

Greer, G. G., and K. Keating. (1977a). What's happening to the American family questionnaire. *Better Homes and Gardens* 55 (9): 125–128.

Greer, G. G., and K. Keating. (1977b). What's happening to the American family questionnaire. *Better Homes and Gardens* 55 (10): 125–128.

Grosskind, F. (1987). American public opinion on poverty, inequality and redistribution programs. Manuscript, University of Michigan.

Handler, J., and Y. Hasenfeld. (1991). *The moral construction of poverty*. Newbury Park, Calif.: Sage.

Harrington, M. (1962). *The other America: Poverty in the United States*. New York: Macmillan.

Harris, L. (1978). *The myth and reality of aging in America*. Washington, D.C.: National Council on Aging.

Heilbroner, R. L. (1970). Benign neglect in the United States. *Transaction* 7 (12): 15–22.

Himmelfarb, G. (1983). *The idea of poverty: England in the early Industrial Age*. New York: Knopf.

Hirschman, A. O. (1982). *Shifting involvements: Private interests and public action*. Princeton: Princeton University Press.

Hochschild, A. (1983). *The managed heart*. Berkeley and Los Angeles: University of California Press.

Hodge, R. W., and D. J. Treiman. (1968). Class identification in the United States. *American Journal of Sociology* 73 (5): 535–547.

Hodgkinson, V., and M. Weitzman. (1992). *Giving and volunteering in the United States*. Washington, D.C.: Independent Sector.

Hollingshead, A., and F. Redlich. (1958). *Social class & mental illness*. New York: Wiley.

Homans, G. C. (1950). *The human group*. New York: Harcourt Brace.

Horner, M. S. (1968). Sex differences in achievement motivation and performance in competitive and non-competitive situations. Ph.D. diss., University of Michigan.

Jaffee, A. J. (1968). William Fielding Ogburn. In *International Encyclopedia of the Social Sciences*, ed. D. Sills. New York: The Free Press.

Jansson, B. (1988). *The reluctant welfare state*. Belmont, Mass.: Wadsworth.

Jencks, C. (1972). *Inequality: A reassessment of the effect of family and schooling in America*. New York: Basic Books.

Karnes, P. D. (1996). Return of the wolf. *Michigan Out-of-Doors*, September, 28–30.

Katz, M. B. (1989). *The undeserving poor: From the war on poverty to the war on welfare*. New York: Pantheon.

Kerner Commission. (1968). *Report of the National Advisory Commission, U.S. National Advisory Commission on Civil Disorders*. Washington, D.C.: U.S. Government Printing Office.

Klebaner, B. (1964). Poverty and its relief in American thought, 1815–61. *Social Service Review* 38 (4): 382–399.

Klein, J. (1994). The politics of promiscuity. *Newsweek*, 16–20.

Lammers, W. W. (1983). *Public policy and the aging*. Washington, D.C.: Congressional Quarterly.

Levy, F. (1988). Growing gap between rich and poor. *New York Times*, May, sec. 3, p. 3.

Lewis, M. (1978). *The culture of inequality*. Amherst: University of Massachusetts Press.

Lind, M. (1995). To have and have not: Notes on the progress of of the American class war. *Harpers*, June, 35–47.

Martin, G. T., Jr., and M. N. Zald, eds. (1981). *Social welfare in society*. New York: Columbia University Press.

Marx. K. (1902). *Capital*. New York: Random House.

May, H. F. (1976). *The enlightenment in America*. New York: Oxford University Press.

McCluskey, N. G., and E. F. Borgatta, eds. (1981). *Aging and retirement: Prospects, planning and policy*. Beverly Hills: Sage.

Merton, R. A. (1957). *Social theory and social structure*. Glencoe, Ill.: The Free Press of Glencoe.

Miller, S. M., and P. Roby. (1976). Strategies for social mobility: A policy framework. In *Strategic perspectives on social policy*, ed. J. E. Tropman, M. Dluhy, R. Lind, W. Vasey, and T. A. Croxton. New York: Pergamon Press. Reprinted from *American Sociologist* 6 (supp., June): 18–22, 1971.

Montgomery, J. D. (1976). Programs and poverty: Federal aid in the domestic and international systems. In *Strategic perspectives on social policy*, ed. J. E. Tropman, M. Dluhy, R. Lind, W. Vasey, and T. A. Croxton. New York: Pergamon Press. Reprinted from *Public Policy* 18 (4): 517–537, 1970.

Morgan, J. N. (1962). *Income and welfare in the United States*. New York: McGraw-Hill.

Moynihan, D. P. (1969). *Maximum feasible misunderstanding: Community action in the war on poverty*. New York: The Free Press.

Myrdal, G. (1962). *An American dilemma: The Negro problem in modern democracy*. 2 vols. New York: Harper & Row.

Myrdal, G. (1944). *An American dilemma: The Negro problem in modern democracy*. New York: Harper & Brothers.

Nam, C. B, M. G. Powers, and P. C. Glick. (1964). Socioeconomic characteristics of the population: 1960. *Current Population Reports*. Series P-23, no. 12: 19, table 3. Washington, D.C.: Bureau of the Census.

Oates, J. C. (1969). *Them*. New York: Vanguard Press.

Ogburn, W. F. (1928). *Social chance with respect to culture and original nature*. New York: Viking.

Palmore, E. B. (1975). *The honorable elders: A cross-cultural analysis of aging in Japan*. Durham, N.C.: Duke University Press.

Parsons, T. (1979). Personal communication with author, March 27.

Passell, P. P. (1996). You saved, but they didn't. So now what? Cracking the baby-boomer nest egg. *New York Times*, 7 July, late New York edition, sec. 3, p. 1.

Perlman, H. H. (1960). Are we creating dependency? *Social Service Review* 34 (3): 323–333.

Peters, T., and R. Waterman. (1982). *In search of excellence: Lessons from America's best-run companies*. New York: Harper & Row.

Plath, D. (1980). *Long engagements: Maturity in modern Japan*. Stanford: Stanford University Press.

Popcorn, F. (1991). *The Popcorn report: Faith Popcorn on the future of your company, your world, your life*. New York: Doubleday.

Rauschenbusch, W. (1911). *Christianity and the social crisis*. New York: Macmillan.

Rawls, J. (1985). Justice as fairness: Political not metaphysical. *Philosophy & Public Affairs* 14 (3): 223–251.

Reisman, D., N. Glazer, and R. Denny. (1956). *The lonely crowd*. New York: Anchor.

Rischin, M. (1965). *The American gospel of success: Individualism and beyond*. Chicago: Quadrangle Books.

Root, L. (1981). Employee benefits and income security: Private social policy and the public interest. In *New strategic perspectives on social policy*, ed. J. E. Tropman, M. Dluhy, and R. Lind. Elmsford, N.Y.: Pergamon Press.

Rothman, S. (1989). Personal communication with author.

Ryan, W. (1971). *Blaming the victim*. New York: Vintage.

Rytina, A. W., W. H. Form, and J. Pease. (1970). Income and stratification ideology: Beliefs about the American opportunity structure. *American Journal of Sociology* 75 (4): 703–716.

Sarri, R. (1970). *Client attributes as seen by agency executives.* Unclassified report, CRD-425-CL-9, Social and Rehabilitation Service, U.S. Department of Health, Education, and Welfare.

Schaef, A. W., and D. Fassel. (1988). *The addictive organization.* San Francisco: Harper & Row.

Schiller, B. R. (1977). Relative earnings mobility in the United States. *American Economic Review* 67 (5): 926–941.

Schiller, B. R. (1973). *The economics of poverty and discrimination.* Englewood Cliffs, N.J.: Prentice Hall.

Schumaker, E. 1973. *Small is beautiful.* London: Blond and Briggs.

Shils, E. (1975). *Center and periphery: Essays in macrosociology.* Chicago: University of Chicago Press.

Silberman, M. (1970). Determinants of felony trials and negotiations. Ph.D. diss., University of Michigan.

Skinner, B. F. (1971). *Beyond freedom and dignity.* New York: Knopf.

Skocpol, T. (1992). *Protecting soldiers and mothers.* Cambridge: Harvard University Press.

Smolensky, E., S. Danziger, and P. Gottschalk. (1988). The declining significance of age: Trends in the well-being of children and the elderly. In *The changing well-being of the aged and children in the United States*, ed. T. Smeeding. Washington, D.C.: Urban Institute Press.

Stack, C. B. (1974). *All our kin: Strategies for survival in a Black community.* New York: Harper & Row.

Tibbitts, C. (1979). Can we invalidate negative stereotypes of aging? *The Gerontologist* 9 (1): 10–20.

Tropman, E. J., and J. E. Tropman. (1987). Voluntary organizations. In *The encyclopedia of social work*, ed. A. Minahan. Silver Spring, Md.: N.A.S.W.

Tropman, J. E. (1995). *The Catholic ethic in American society.* San Francisco: Jossey Bass.

Tropman, J. E. (1989). *American values and social welfare: Cultural contradictions in the welfare state.* Englewood Cliffs, N.J.: Prentice Hall.

Tropman, J. E. (1987). *Public policy opinion and the elderly.* Westport, Conn.: Greenwood Press.

Tropman, J. E. (1986). The "Catholic ethic" versus the "Protestant ethic": Catholic social service and the welfare state. *Social Thought* 12 (1): 13–22.

Tropman, J. E. (1976). Public welfare: Utilization, change appropriations, service. *Journal of Sociology and Welfare* 3 (3): 264–290.

Tropman, J. E. (1974). *A guide to advocacy for area planners in aging.* Ann Arbor: Michigan Project TAP.

Tropman, J., and A. L. Gordon. (1978). The welfare threat: AFDC coverage and closeness in the American states. *Social Forces* 57 (2): 697–712.

Tropman, J. E., and J. Strate. (1983). Social characteristics and personal opinion: Notes toward a theory. *California Sociologist* 6 (1): 23–38.

Tuchman, B. (1978). *Distant mirror: The calamitous 14th century.* New York: Knopf.

Turner, R. H. (1960). Sponsored and contest mobility and the school system. *American Sociological Review* 25 (6): 855–867.

Urban America. (1969). *One year later: An assessment of the nation's response to the crisis described by the National Advisory Commission on Civil Disorders.* New York: Praeger.

U.S. Bureau of the Census. (1996). *Statistical abstract of the United States: 1996.* 116th ed. Washington, D.C.: Author.

Vidich, A. J., and J. Bensman. (1968). *Small town in mass society.* Princeton: Princeton University Press.

Warner, W. 1. (1949). *Democracy in Jonesville.* New York: Harper & Brothers.

Williamson, J. R. (1974a). Beliefs about the motivation of the poor and attitudes toward poverty policy. *Social Problems* 21 (5): 634–648.

Williamson, J. R. (1974b). Beliefs about the welfare poor. *Sociology and Social Research* 58 (2): 163–175.

Wolfensberger, W. (1972). *The principles of normalization in the human services.* Toronto: Leonard/Crawford National Institute of Mental Retardation.

Yinger, J. M. (1982). *Countercultures: The promise and the peril of a world turned upside down.* New York: The Free Press.

Zeldich, M., Jr. (1968). Status, Social. In *International encyclopedia of the social sciences,* ed. David L. Sills. Vol. 15. New York: Macmillan and The Free Press.

Bibliography

Abramovitz, M. Putting an end to doublespeak about race, gender, and poverty: An annotated glossary for social workers. *Social Work* 36 (1988): 380–384.

Abramovitz, M. *Regulating the lives of women*. Boston: South End Press, 1988.

Abramovitz, M., and F. F. Piven. Scapegoating women on welfare. *New York Times*, 2 September 1993.

Adams, B. *The law of civilization and decay*. New York: Vintage Books, 1955.

Ager, S. Affluence guilt. *Detroit Free Press*, 9 February 1993, 3f.

Allport, G. *Religion in the developing personality*. New York: New York University Press, 1960.

Alston, J. P., and K. I. Dean. Socioeconomic factors associated with attitudes toward welfare recipients and causes of poverty. *Social Service Review* 46 (1971): 13–23.

Alves, W. M., and P. H. Rossi. Who should get what? Fairness judgments of the distribution of earnings. *American Journal of Sociology* 84 (1978): 541–564.

Alwin, D. *Religion and parental child rearing orientations*. Manuscript, University of Michigan, 1985.

Amenta, E., and B. Carruthers. The formative years of U.S. social spending policies. *American Sociological Review* 53 (1988): 661–678.

America's needy: Care and cutbacks: Timely reports to keep journalists, scholars, and the public abreast of developing issues, events, and trends. Washington, D.C.: Congressional Quarterly, 1984.

Aponte, H. J. *Bread and spirit: Therapy with the new poor—Diversity of race, culture, and values*. New York: Norton, 1994.

Apter, M. *The experience of motivation*. New York: Academic Press, 1982.

Ashford, D. *The emergence of the welfare states*. New York: Basil Blackwell, 1986.

Associated Press. Report on who's bound for Hell bedevils baptists. *Ann Arbor News*, 19 September 1993, 1.

Axinn, J. M., and A. E. Hirsch. Welfare and the "reform" of women. *Families in Society: The Journal of Contemporary Human Services* 22 (1993): 563–572.

Axinn, J., and M. J. Stern. Age and dependency: Children and the aged in American social policy. *Health and Society* 63 (1985): 648–670.

Bane, M. J., and D. Ellwood. *Welfare realities*. Cambridge: Harvard University Press, 1994.

Barry, B. D., Jr. Some issues in the proper study of Black America. In *American character and culture in a changing world*, ed. J. Hague. Westport, Conn.: Greenwood Press, 1979.

Bellah, R. et al. *Habits of the heart: Individualism and commitment in American life*. New York: Perennial Library, 1986.

Bellah, R. *Tokugawa religion: The cultural roots of modern Japan*. New York: The Free Press, 1957.

Bellah, R., and P. Hammond. *Varieties of civil religion*. San Francisco: Harper & Row, 1980.

Bem, D. *Beliefs, attitudes, and human affairs*. Belmont: Brooks/Cole, 1970.

Benedict, R. *Patterns of culture*. Boston: Houghton Mifflin. 1934.

Berger, P. L. Can the bishops help the poor? *Commentary* 79 (1985): 31–35.

Berger, P. L. *The concept of economic culture*. Manuscript, New York.

Berger, P. L. *The noise at solemn assemblies: Christian commitment and the religious establishment in America*. Garden City, N.Y.: Doubleday, 1961.

Beveridge, Sir Wm. *Social insurance and allied services*. New York: Macmillan, 1942.

Bishop, K. Vouchers place money in the hands of the needy, instead of the greedy. *New York Times*, 26 July 1991, 2.

Bogardus, E. S. *Essentials of Americanization*. Los Angeles: University of Southern California Press, 1919.

Boorstin, D. J. *The Americans: The colonial experience*. New York: Random House, 1958.

Boorstin, D. J. *The Americans: The democratic experience*. New York: Random House, 1973.

Boorstin, D. J. *The Americans: The national experience*. New York: Random House, 1965.

Boulding, K. E. The boundaries of social policy. *Social Work* 12 (1967): 3–11.

Brace, C. L. *The dangerous classes of New York and twenty years work among them*. New York: Wynkoop and Hallenbeck, 1872.

Bremmer, R. H. *American philanthropy*. Chicago: University of Chicago Press, 1960.

Brenner, M. H. *Mental illness and the economy*. Cambridge: Harvard University Press, 1973.

Brinkley, A. *Voices of protest: Huey Long, Father Coughlin and the Great Depression*. New York: Vintage Books, 1982.

Broderick, R. C., ed. *The Catholic encyclopedia*. New York: Nelson, 1987.

Cameron, C. *Attitudes of the poor and attitudes toward the poor: An annotated bibliography*. Suppl. 1. Madison: Institute for Research on Poverty, University of Wisconsin, 1977.

Clark, W. F. *Old and poor: A critical assessment of the low income elderly*. Lexington, Mass.: Lexington Books, 1988.

Cleary, E. L., ed. *Born of the poor: The Latin American church since medellin.* Notre Dame, Ind.: University of Notre Dame Press, 1990.

Cochran, T. C. *Challenges to American values: Society, business, religion.* New York: Oxford University Press, 1985.

Copeland, W. A. *And the poor get welfare: The ethics of poverty in the United States.* Nashville: Abington Press, 1994.

Cross, F. L., and W. A. Livingstone, eds. *The Oxford dictionary of the Christian church.* 2d ed. New York: Oxford University Press, 1990.

Cross, R. D. *The emergence of liberal Catholicism in America.* Cambridge: Harvard University Press, 1958.

Croxton, T., and J. E. Tropman. The new puritans? In *Behaviorism and ethics,* ed. J. E. Krapfl and E. Vargas. Kalamazoo: Behaviordelia, 1977.

Cumming, E., and W. E. Henry. (1961). *Growing old.* New York: Basic Books.

Curran, C. Ethical principles of Catholic social teaching behind the United States Bishops' letter on the economy. *Journal of Business Ethics* 7 (1988): 413–417.

D'Antonio, W. V., J. D. Davidson, and J. A. Schlanger. *Protestants and Catholics in two Oklahoma communities.* South Bend: University of Notre Dame, Department of Sociology, 1965.

D'Antonio, W. V., D. Hoge, and R. Wallace. *American Catholic laity in a changing church.* Kansas City, Mo.: Sheed and Ward, 1989.

Danziger, S., and P. Gottschalk. *America unequal.* Cambridge: Harvard University Press, 1995.

Danziger, S., G. Sandfur, and D. H. Weinberg, eds. *Confronting poverty: Prescriptions for change.* New York: Russell Sage Foundation, 1994.

Danziger, S., and D. H. Weinberg. *Poverty.* Cambridge: Harvard University Press, 1986.

Davidson, J. D. Glock's model of religious commitment. *Review of Religious Research* 16 (1972): 83–92.

Deaton, A. *Measuring poverty among the elderly.* Cambridge: National Bureau of Economic Research.

Degler, C. N. *In search of human nature: The decline and revival of Darwinism in American social thought.* New York: Oxford University Press, 1990.

De Hartog, J. *The peaceable kingdom.* New York: Atheneum Publishers, 1971.

Desan, P. Thinking in market terms. *University of Chicago Magazine,* October 1993, 8–9.

Desmet, K. The private penance of Tom Monaghan. *Detroit Free Press,* 17 November 1991, 1.

Door, D. *The social justice agenda.* Maryknoll, N.Y.: Orbis, 1991.

Dubois, E. Almsgiving in postreformation England. *History of European Ideas* 9 (1988): 489–495.

Duncan, G., and M. Hill. Attitudes, behaviors, and economic outcomes. In *Five thousand American families,* Vol. 3, ed. G. Duncan and J. Morgan. Ann Arbor: Institute of Social Research, 1975.

Durkheim, E. *The division of labor in society.* Glencoe, Ill.: Free Press of Glencoe, 1960.

Durkheim, E. The dualism of human nature and its social conditions. In *Emile Durkheim, 1858–1917: A collection of essays,* trans. C. Blend, ed. K. H. Wolff. Columbus: Ohio State University Press, 1960.

Durkheim, E. *Suicide*, translated and with an introduction by J. A. Spaulding and G. Simpson. Glencoe, Ill.: Free Press of Glencoe, 1951.

Eckardt, R. *Black–woman–Jew: Three wars for human liberation*. Bloomington: Indiana University Press, 1986.

Edelman, M. *Political language: Words that succeed and policies that fail*. New York: Academic Press, 1977.

Ehrenreich, B. *The hearts of men: American dreams and the flight from commitment*. Garden City, N.Y.: Anchor Press, 1983.

Erickson, E. *Childhood and society*. New York: Norton, 1950.

Erikson, K. *Everything in its path: Destruction of community in the Buffalo Creek flood*. New York: Simon & Schuster, 1976.

Feagin, J. R. *Subordinating the poor: Welfare and American beliefs*. Englewood Cliffs, N.J.: Prentice Hall, 1975.

Fischer, F. *Politics, values and public policy*. Boulder: Westview Press, 1980.

Frankel, M. What the poor deserve: View of H. J. Gans. *New York Times Magazine*, 22 October 1995, 46.

Fraser, N., and L. Gordon. A genealogy of dependency. *Signs: Journal of Women in Culture and Society* 19 (1994): 309–333.

Funciello, T. *Tyranny of kindness: Dismantling the welfare system to end poverty in America*. New York: Atlantic Monthly Press, 1993.

Galbraith, J. K. *The culture of contentment*. Boston: Houghton Mifflin, 1922.

Gans, H. J. *The war against the poor: The underclass and antipoverty policy*. New York: Basic Books, 1995.

Geertz, C. Blurred genres: The refiguration of social thought. *The American Scholar* 49 (1980): 165–179.

Gilbert, N. *Capitalism and the welfare state: Dilemmas of social benevolence*. New Haven: Yale University Press, 1983.

Gilder, G. *Wealth and poverty*. New York: Basic Books, 1981.

Ginzberg, L. *Women and the work of benevolence: Morality, politics and class in the 19th century United States*. New Haven: Yale University Press, 1990.

Girvetz, H. Welfare state. In *International encyclopedia of the social sciences*, Vol. 16, ed. David L. Sills. New York: Macmillan and The Free Press, 1968.

Gordon, L. *Pitied but not entitled: Single mothers and the history of welfare (1890–1935)*. New York: The Free Press, 1994.

Gordon, L., ed. The new feminist scholarship on the welfare state. In *Women, the state, and welfare*. Madison: University of Wisconsin Press, 1990.

Gorrell, D. K. *The age of social responsibility: The social gospel in the progressive era, 1900–1920*. Macon, Ga.: Mercer University Press, 1988.

Greeley, A. M. *The Catholic myth: The behavior and beliefs of American Catholics*. New York: Scribners, 1990.

Greenberg, M. R. *Environmentally devastated neighborhoods: Perceptions, policies, and realities*. New Brunswick, N.J.: Rutgers University Press, 1996.

Gronbjerg, K. A. *Mass society and the extension of welfare, 1960–1970*. Chicago: University of Chicago Press, 1977.

Handler, J. F. *The poverty of welfare reform*. New Haven: Yale University Press, 1995.

Hartz, L. *The liberal tradition in America: An interpretation of American political thought since the revolution*. New York: Harcourt, Brace, 1955.

Hawley, A. H. *Human ecology*. New York: Ronald Press, 1950.

Hill, M. S. *Motivation and economic mobility*. Ann Arbor: Survey Research Center, 1985.

Himmelfarb, G. *The de-moralization of society: From Victorian virtues to modern values*. New York: Knopf, 1995.

Himmelfarb, G. *Points of light: New approaches to ending welfare dependency*. Washington, D.C.: Ethics and Public Policy Center, 1991.

Himmelfarb, G. *Poverty and compassion: The moral imagination of the late Victorians*. New York: Knopf, 1991.

Hirschman, A. O. *Exit, voice, and loyalty: Responses to decline in firms, organizations, and states*. Cambridge: Harvard University Press, 1970.

Hoff, M. Response to the Catholic bishops letter on the economy. *Social Thought* (Winter 1989): 41–52.

Hofstadter, R. *The age of reform*. New York: Vintage, 1955.

Hofstede, G. *Culture's consequences: International differences in work-related values*. Beverly Hills: Sage, 1980.

Hollenbach, D. *Claims in conflict*. New York: Paulist Press, 1979.

Holt, A. E. *Social work in the churches: A study in the practice of fellowship*. Boston: Pilgrim Press, 1922.

Horowitz, I. I. *Winners and losers: Social and political polarities in America*. Durham, N.C.: Duke University Press, 1984.

Hudson, R. B. The "graying" of the federal budget, and its consequences for old age policy. In *New strategic perspectives on social policy*, ed. J. E. Tropman, M. Dluhy, and R. Lind. Elmsford, N.Y.: Pergamon Press, 1981.

Inglehart, R. *Culture shift*. Princeton: Princeton University Press, 1990.

Johansen, E. *Comparable worth: The myth and the movement*. Boulder: Westview Press, 1984.

Johnson, W. *Muddling toward frugality*. Boulder: Shambhala, 1979.

Kahn, A. J., ed. *Issues in American social work*. New York: Columbia University Press, 1959.

Kallen, D. J., and D. Miller. Public attitudes toward welfare. *Social Work* 16 (1971): 83–90.

Kammer, F. S. J. *Doing faith justice: An introduction to Catholic social thought*. New York: Paulist Press, 1991.

Katz, D. *Bureaucratic encounters: A pilot study in the evaluation of government services*. Ann Arbor: Institute for Social Research, University of Michigan, 1975.

Katz, M. B. *Improving poor people: The welfare state, the "underclass," and urban schools as history*. Princeton: Princeton University Press, 1995.

Katz, M. B. The undeserving poor. *Women's Review of Books* (March 1990): 7.

Kelso, W. A. *Poverty and the underclass: Changing perceptions of the poor in America*. New York: New York University Press, 1994.

Kennedy, R. J. R. Single or triple melting-pot intermarriage trends in New Haven, 1870–1940. *American Journal of Sociology* 49 (1944): 331–339.

Kersten, L. L. *The Lutheran ethic: The impact of religion on laymen and clergy*. Detroit: Wayne State University Press, 1970.

Killinger, B. *Workaholics: The respectable addiction*. E. Roseville, N.Y.: Simon & Schuster, 1992.

Kirschner, D. S. *The paradox of professionalism: Reform and public service in urban America, 1900–1940*. Westport, Conn.: Greenwood Press, 1986.

Knadler, A. Help seeking as a cultural phenomenon: Differences between city and kibbutz dwellers. *Journal of Personality and Social Psychology* 51 (1986): 976–982.

Kohn, A. *No contest*. Boston: Houghton Mifflin, 1986.

Kushner, H. S. *When bad things happen to good people*. New York: Avon, 1983.

Ladd, E. C. Americans at work. *Public Opinion* 4 (August–September 1981): 21–40.

Lawrence, W. The relation of wealth to morals. In *Democracy and the gospel of wealth*, ed. G. Kennedy. Boston: Heath, 1948.

Leacock, E. B. *The culture of poverty: A critique*. New York: Simon & Schuster, 1971.

Leiby, J. Moral foundations of social welfare and social work: A historical view. *Social Work* 30 (1985): 323–330.

Lewis, O. The culture of poverty. *Scientific American* 215 (1966): 19–25.

Linder, R. *The fifty-minute hour: A collection of psychoanalytic tales*. New York: Rinehart, 1954.

Lipset, S. M. *The first new nation*. New York: Basic Books, 1963.

Longman, P. Taking America to the cleaners. *Washington Monthly*, November 1982, 24–30.

Magnet, M. *The dream and the nightmare: The sixties' legacy to the underclass*. New York: Morrow, 1993.

Malinowsky, B. *Magic, science and religion and other essays*. Selected and with an introduction by Robert Redfield. Boston: Beacon Press, 1948.

March, J. G., and H. Simon. *Organizations*. New York: Wiley, 1958.

Marciniac, E. Toward a Catholic work ethic. *Origins*, 25 February 1988, 631–637.

Maxwell, A. H. The underclass, "social isolation" and "concentration effects." *Critique of Anthropology* 13 (1993): 231–244.

McCarthy, E., and W. McGaughey. *Nonfinancial economics: The case for shorter hours of work*. New York: Praeger, 1989.

McGregor, D. *The human side of enterprise*. New York: McGraw-Hill, 1960.

McJimsey, G. *Harry Hopkins: Ally of the poor and defender of democracy*. Cambridge: Harvard University Press, 1987.

Mead, L. M. *Beyond entitlement: The social obligations of citizenship*. New York: The Free Press, 1986.

Mead, L. M. Poverty policy and the poverty of policy toward the poor. *Policy Studies Journal* 23 (1995): 162–164.

Meltzer, M. *Poverty in America*. New York: Morrow, 1986.

Miller, W. B. Implications of urban lower-class culture for social work. *Social Service Review* 33 (1959): 219–236.

Miller, W. C. *A handbook of American minorities*. New York: New York University Press, 1976.

Miller, W. D. *Dorothy Day*. New York: Harper & Row, 1982.

Mills, C. W. *The power elite*. New York: Oxford University Press, 1956.

Mooney, C. F. *Public virtue: Law and the social character of religion*. Notre Dame, Ind.: University of Notre Dame Press, 1986.

Moynihan, D. P. *The Negro family: The case for national action*. Washington, D.C.: Department of Labor, Office of Planning and Research, 1965.

Murray, C. *Loosing ground: American social policy, 1950–1980*. New York: Basic Books, 1984.

Murray, H. *Do not neglect hospitality: The Catholic worker and the homeless*. Philadelphia: Temple University Press, 1990.

Nadler, A. Help seeking as cultural phenomenon. *American Psychologist* 52 (1986): 976–982.

Naisbitt, J. *Megatrends: Ten new directions for transforming our lives*. New York: Warner, 1982.

Nash, R. H. *Poverty and wealth: The Christian debate over capitalism*. Westchester, Ill.: Good News/Crossway, 1986.

NCCB. *Economic justice for all: Pastoral letter on Catholic social teaching and the U.S. economy*. Washington, D.C.: United States Catholic Conference, 1986.

Neugarten, B., ed. *Age or need? Future public policies for older people*. Beverly Hills: Sage, 1982.

Newman, K. *Falling from grace: The experience of downward mobility in the American middle class*. New York: The Free Press, 1986.

Novak, M. *The Catholic ethic and the spirit of capitalism*. New York: The Free Press, 1993.

Nussbaum, M. Recoiling from reason. *New York Review*, 7 December 1989, 36–41.

Odendahl, T. *Charity begins at home: Generosity and self-interest among the philanthropic elite*. New York: Basis Books, 1990.

O'Grady, J. *Catholic charities in the United States*. Washington, D.C.: National Conference of Catholic Charities, 1930.

Organization for Economic Cooperation and Development (OECD). *The welfare state in crisis*. Paris: OECD, 1981.

Orloff, A. S., and T. Skocpol. Why not equal protection: Explaining the politics of public social spending. *American Sociological Review* 49 (1984): 726–750.

Ouchi, W. *Theory Z*. New York: Bantam, 1981.

Palmer, P. J. *The active life*. New York: Harper & Row, 1990.

Palmer, P. J. *To know as we are known*. San Francisco: HarperCollins, 1983.

Palmer, P. J. Scarcity, abundance, and the gift of community. *Community Renewal Press* 1 (1990): 2–6.

Parsons, T. Anglo American society. In *International encyclopedia of the social sciences*, Vol. 2, ed. David L. Sills. New York: Macmillan and The Free Press, 1968.

Parsons, T. Christianity. In *International encyclopedia of the social sciences*, Vol. 2, ed. David L. Sills. New York: Macmillan and The Free Press, 1968.

Parsons, T., and R. F. Bales. *Family: Socialization and interaction process*. Glencoe, Ill.: Free Press of Glencoe, 1955.

Pascale, R. T., and A. G. Athos. *The art of Japanese management*. New York: Simon & Schuster, 1981.

Paul, J. II. *On human work*. Washington, D.C.: United States Catholic Conference, 1981.

Piven, F. F. *The new class war: Reagan's attack on the welfare state and its consequences*. New York: Pantheon, 1982.

Piven, F. F., and R. A. Cloward. *Regulating the poor: The function of public welfare*. New York: Pantheon, 1971.

Pumphrey, R. E., and M. W. Pumphrey, eds. *The heritage of American social work*. New York: Columbia University Press, 1961.

Quadango, J. S. Welfare capitalism and the Social Security Act of 1935. *American Sociological Review* 49 (1984): 445–446.

Quatrochocchi, S. Fringe benefits as private social policy. In *New strategic perspectives on social policy*, ed. J. E. Tropman, M. Dluhy, and R. Lind. Elmsford, N.Y.: Pergamon Press, 1981.

Quinn, R. *Beyond rational management*. San Francisco: Jossey Bass, 1989.

Redmont., J. *Regulating the poor: The functions of public welfare*. New York: Pantheon, 1971.

Reich, R. *The next American frontier*. New York: Times Books, 1983.

Roberts, K. *Religion in sociological perspective*. 2d ed. Belmont, Calif.: Wadsworth, 1990.

Rokeach, M. *Beliefs, attitudes and values*. San Francisco: Jossey Bass, 1968.

Rokeach, M. Part 1: Value systems and religion. *Review of Religious Research* 11 (1969): 1–23.

Rokeach, M. Part 2: Religious values and social compassion. *Review of Religious Research* 11 (1969): 24–39.

Rothman, D. J., and S. Wheeler, eds. *Social history and social policy*. New York: Academic Press, 1981.

Rotter, J. Generalized expectancies for internal versus external control of reinforcement. *Psychological Monographs* 80 (1966).

Russell, J. R. *The devil: Perceptions of evil from antiquity to primitive Christianity*. Ithaca: Cornell University Press, 1977.

Ryan, W. *Equality*. New York: Pantheon, 1981.

Ryle, E. J. Attitudes toward the poor and public policy development. In *Justice and health care*, ed. M. J. Kelly. St. Louis: Catholic Health Care Association of the U.S., 1985.

Ryle, E. J. Catholic social thought and the New Federalism. *Center Journal* 2 (1983): 9–36.

Ryle, E. J. Option for the poor in Catholic charities: Policy and the social teaching of John Paul II. *Social Thought* Spring–Summer (1987): 139–149.

Sachar, H. M. *The course of modern Jewish history*. Rev. ed. New York: Vintage, 1990.

Sampson, E. E. The decentralization of identity: Toward a revised concept of personal and social order. *American Psychologist* 40 (1985): 1203–1211.

Saveth, E. Patrician philanthropy in America: The late nineteenth and early twentieth centuries. *Social Service Review* 54 (1980): 76–91.

Schein, V. *Working from the margins: Voices of mothers in poverty*. Ithaca: Cornell University Press, 1995.

Schlesinger, A. M., Jr. *The Age of Roosevelt, Vol. 1: The crisis of the old order, 1919–1933*. Boston: Houghton Mifflin, 1957.

Schrag, P. *The decline of the WASP*. New York: Simon & Schuster, 1970.

Sen, A. Individual freedom as a social commitment. *New York Review*, 14 June 1990, 49–54.

Shapiro, H. T. Philanthropy: Tradition and change. In *Tradition and change*, ed. H. Shapiro. Ann Arbor: University of Michigan Press, 1987.

Shapiro, H. T. The Jewish tradition of charity: Remarks at the closing celebration of the 1982 allied Jewish campaign—Israel emergency fund. Manuscript, University of Michigan, 1982.

Skocpol, T. *Social policy in the United States*. Princeton: Princeton University Press, 1995.

Slater, P. E. *The pursuit of loneliness: American culture at the breaking point*. Boston: Beacon Press, 1970.

Smith, H. *The religions of man*. New York: Harper & Row and Perennial Library, 1986.

The statistical history of the United States, from colonial times to the present. New York: Horizon Press, 1965.

Stein, J. *Fiddler on the roof*. New York: Washington Square Press, 1964.

Stinchcomb, A. J. Social structure in organizations. In *Handbook of organizations*, ed. J. G. March. Chicago: Rand McNally, 1965.

Tawney, R. H. *The acquisitive society*. New York: Harcourt, Brace, 1948.

Tawney, R. H. *Religion and the rise of Capitalism*. London: Murray, 1926.

Thurow, L. *Head to head*. New York: Morrow, 1992.

Tichy, N., and M. A. Devanna. *The transformational leader*. New York: Wiley, 1986.

Tocqueville, A. de. *Democracy in America*. Vols. 1 and 2. New York: Random House, 1945.

Tönnies, F. *Community and Society—Gemeinschaft und Gesellschaft*. 2d ed. Trans. C. P. Loomis. East Lansing: Michigan State University Press,1957.

Tropman, J. E. Copping out or chipping in. *The Humanist* 41 (1981): 43–46.

Tropman, J. E., and G. Morningstar. *Entrepreneurial systems for the 1990s*. Westport, Conn.: Quorum Books, 1989.

Tropman, J. E., and J. Strate. Social characteristics and personal opinion: Notes toward a theory. *California Sociologist* 6 (1983): 23–38.

Valentine, C. A. *Culture and poverty: Critique and counter-proposals*. Chicago: University of Chicago Press, 1968.

Vladeck, B. C. *Voices from the Catholic worker*. Philadelphia: Temple University Press, 1993.

Wald, K. *Religion and politics in the United States*. New York: St. Martin's Press, 1987.

Wallace, R. The secular ethic and the spirit of patriotism. *Sociological Analysis* 34 (1973): 3–11.

Waterman, A. S. Individualism and interdependence. *The American Psychologist* 36 (1981): 762–773.

Watson, S. Feast and famine shade marriage. *Detroit Free Press*, 9 August 1991.

Weber, M. *From Max Weber*. Trans. H. Gearth and C. W. Mills. New York: Oxford University Press, 1946.

Weber, M. *The Protestant ethic in the spirit of Capitalism*. Trans. T. Parsons. New York: Charles Scribner's Sons, 1956.

Weber, M. *The sociology of religion*. Trans. E. Fischoff. New York: Beacon Press, 1963.

Weicher, J. C., ed. *Maintaining the safety net: Income redistribution programs in the Reagan administration*. Washington, D.C.: American Enterprise Institute, 1984.

Welch, W. States forging ahead on welfare reform. *USA Today*, 13 August 1993.

Wilensky, H. L. Leftism, Catholicism, and democratic corporatism: The role of political parties in recent welfare state development. In *The development of welfare states in Europe and America*, ed. P. Flora and A. J. Heidenheimer. New Brunswick, N.J.: Transaction Books, 1981.

Wilensky, H. L., and C. Lebeaux. *Industrial society and social welfare: The impact of industrialization on the supply and organization of social welfare services in the United States*. New York: Russell Sage Foundation, 1958.

Will, G. A sterner kind of caring. *Newsweek*, 13 January 1992, 68.

Will, J. R. *The deserving poor*. New York: Garland, 1993.

Williams, R. M, Jr. *American society*. 2d ed. New York: Knopf, 1960.

Wines, M. Not my job, not our job: So whose job is it? *New York Times*, 9 April 1995, sec. 4, p. 1.

Wollack, S., et al. Development of the survey of work values. *Journal of Applied Psychology* 53 (1971): 331–338.

Wood, J. R. *Leadership in voluntary organizations: The controversy over social action in Protestant churches*. New Brunswick: Rutgers University Press, 1981.

Woodward, K. L. Encountering Mary. *New York Times Book Review*, 11 August 1991, 1ff.

Wortman, C. Causal attributions and personal control. In *New directions in attribution research*, Vol 1, ed. J. Harvey and W. J. Ickes. Hillsdale, N.J.: Erlbaum, 1976.

Wright, R. G. *Does the law morally bind the poor, or, what good's the Constitution when you can't buy a loaf of bread?* New York: New York University Press, 1996.

Wuthnow, R. *Acts of compassion*. Princeton: Princeton University Press, 1991.

Wuthnow, R. *Communities of discourse*. Cambridge: Harvard University Press, 1989.

Yankelovich, D. *New rules*. New York: Random House, 1981.

Yankelovich, D., and J. Immerwahr. *Putting the work ethic to work*. New York: Public Agenda Foundation, 1983.

Yankelovich, D., and J. Immerwahr. Putting the work ethic to work. *Society* 21 (1984): 58–76.

Zangwill, I. *The melting pot*. New York: Macmillan, 1922.

Index

ABOUT THE AUTHOR

JOHN E. TROPMAN is Professor of Social Policy, School of Social Work, University of Michigan. Among Professor Tropman's earlier publications are *Public Policy Opinion and the Elderly, 1952–1978* (Greenwood Press, 1987), *Entrepreneurial Systems for the 1990s* with Gersh Morningstar (Quorum Books, 1989), and *The Management of Ideas in the Creating Organization* (Quorum Books, 1998).

ISBN 0-275-96132-X

EAN

9 780275 961329

90000>

HARDCOVER BAR CODE